AS THE
FAMILY
GOES, SO GOES THE
NATION

AS THE
FAMILY
GOES, SO GOES THE
NATION

Principles and Practices for
Building Healthy Families

ELIZABETH L. YOUMANS, ED.D.

JILL C. THRIFT, PH.D.

SCOTT D. ALLEN

Dedication

We dedicate this book to Danny Apparao Adames; his parents, Smita Donthamsetty and Danny Johel Adames; our children and grandchildren; and the future generations of youth around the world. May they learn these principles as children and thereby contribute to the healing of their nations.

As Americans, our legacy is one of Christian character and conscience imparted to youth in the family. Our prayer is that God will bring reformation to Christian families and through them restore our beloved nation to her Christian foundation.

Righteousness exalts a nation,
But sin is a disgrace to any people.
(Proverbs 14:34)

CONTENTS

ABOUT THE COVER

The pomegranate tree with birds has biblical significance. It brings to mind Psalm 1, which likens the righteous man "whose delight is in the law of the Lord" to a fruitful, prosperous tree "whose leaf does not wither." It also echoes Jesus' parable of the kingdom of God, which He compares to a mustard seed that grows into a mighty tree and provides protection and nourishment to the birds of the air (Matthew 13:31–32).

Jewish tradition teaches that the pomegranate is a symbol of righteousness because it is said to have 613 seeds, which correspond to the 613 commandments of the Torah. In Scripture, a seed represents complete provision because it contains all that is needed for the reproduction of life. Likewise, a principle is like a seed. It will reproduce its truth in righteous thought and practice.

A person's life is said to be of greater value than the birds that are clothed and fed by Father God. Parents need not be anxious for their young, they need only to seek first God's kingdom and His righteousness, and provision will be made for all that pertains to life and godliness (Matthew 6:26–33; 1 Peter 1:3). These are themes that all deeply relate to the topic of this book: building fruitful, flourishing families based on the Word of God.

PREFACE

The seed idea for this book was inspired in 2007 by requests from Latin American parents whose children were enrolled in our AMO® Programs. Having witnessed remarkable changes in their children's behavior, speech, and interests, they asked us for a resource that would teach them the same Bible-based truths their children were learning. The idea expanded in a discussion I had with Scott Allen, president of Disciple Nations Alliance, to include principles of godly marriage and parenting. DNA and Chrysalis are international ministries operating from the same Christian school of thought. DNA teaches the strategic role of local churches in social and cultural transformation, and Chrysalis teaches God's place of education in discipling nations. Both are teaching and equipping ministries with similar core beliefs, and both disciple church and community leaders for cultural and social transformation. Our discussion prompted collaboration on a book that would serve the mission of both ministries. We invited our colleague, educator Jill Thrift, to share in the writing. You will hear three distinct voices throughout the chapters but one complementary message. We believe the book is richer by our joint labor and pray that God will use it as a tool for building healthy families in the Body of Christ around the world.

ELIZABETH L. YOUMANS

INTRODUCTION

The modern family is in crisis in the nations of the world. The family as God established it is largely in collapse. Marriage and the nuclear family have been redefined in the twenty-first century, while the global culture of death disciples our children. By culture is meant the historical setting and social context of ideas and habits within which the Church proclaims and lives the gospel of Christ. Where is the influence of the biblical family in our culture? Where is the light of Jesus Christ in our institutions? Why is the Church not in the forefront, discipling our nations? It appears that the Church is held captive by the postmodern culture, and her indifference to its cultural context contributes to its spread within the Church and the family. Sadly, many Christian families are eroded by this influence and offer little contrast to secular families. The war today is both spiritual and cultural—a war of ideas and habits waged by Satan on the battleground of the believer's heart and mind. It is a contest over the guiding ideas and habits of mind and heart that inform the way we understand the world and our place in it.

God established the family as the bedrock of society, the basic building block of nations. Out of the twelve tribes descended from Abraham's family, He raised up a mighty nation amidst the dark culture and idolatry of those around them. He gave His chosen people His moral and ceremonial laws with which to build a godly culture. He consecrated His people and set Israel apart to be a light among the Gentile nations, so that His salvation might reach the ends of the earth (Isaiah 46:6). God commissioned *parents* to impart this godly heritage to the next generation through their lives and their teaching. But they yearned to be like the pagan nations that surrounded them and exchanged God's truth for a lie. During one time of great moral decline, Jeremiah challenged them to return to God's ancient pathway:

> *Thus says the Lord, "Stand by the ways and see and ask for the ancient paths, where the good way is, and walk in it; and you will find rest for your souls." But they said, "We will not walk in it."* (Jeremiah 6:16)

The Role of the Church in Discipling the Nation

Healthy families produce healthy nations. Healthy families are the fruit of intentional, biblical teaching and practice of God's purpose and principles for both marriage and parenting. This is the role of the Church—to equip families with consistent, sound Christian teaching so they can be salt and light in their communities. As John Calvin preached and taught God's Word to his church families during the 1500s, line upon line, precept upon precept, he initiated a "family reformation." His ability to articulate the majesty of God and the sufficiency of Scripture for every area of family life birthed a Reformation that not only affected the city of Geneva and all its institutions but also transformed the nations of northern Europe and greatly influenced the ideals and lifestyle of the founding families of the United States. Known as "the people of the Book," the Pilgrims and Puritans traveled west across the Atlantic to establish a culture in which biblical principles would govern family and community life. When God's people return to His ancient ways and apply biblical principles to personal and family life, individuals, families, communities, and nations are transformed.

Recovering a Vision for the Family in Discipling Healthy Nations

Today, the Church has to a great degree lost this vision. Christianity no longer challenges the habits of the heart and mind with Christian doctrine but is dominated by the prevailing habits of thought and practice of the surrounding culture. We are deceived into believing that the ancient pathway is irrelevant to modernity, and that the lifestyle and preaching of a John Calvin or Martin Luther are disconnected from our complex, postmodern issues. Nothing could be further from the truth! Jesus Christ is the same yesterday, today, and forever (Hebrews 13:8). His Word is alive, active, and sharper than a two-edged sword. God's wisdom and ways have not changed, and His living, eternal Word remains potent with sure answers for today's challenges.

Where there is no vision, the people perish (Proverbs 29:18). This impoverishment is evident throughout Christianity. Many Christian families live in brokenness and despair. The vast majority of children from Christian families are educated in state schools that teach an anti-Christian world and life view. Parents lack a biblical vision for wholeness in marriage and family life and relegate the spiritual education of their children to outsiders. Our nations cry out for the light of Scripture to transform both heart and home:

> Make us know Thy ways, O Lord; Teach us Thy paths.
> Lead us in Thy truth and teach us,
>   for Thou art the God of our salvation;
> Remember Thy compassion and Thy lovingkindnesses,
>   For they have been from of old . . .

All the paths of the Lord are lovingkindness and truth
To those who keep His covenant and His testimonies.
(Psalm 25:4–9)

A Primer of Principles and Practices

This book is a definitive work written for the families around the world with whom we have relationships. It is a primer, a "first-book" that seeks to both challenge the reader's worldview and inspire the reader to reason with the revelation of God's Word and apply truth to his life. Each chapter poses questions, suggests applications, and provides doable assignments to encourage real change. Therefore, it could be used in one's private devotional time or as a husband and wife or small group study.

The content is presented by principles. A principle is a foundational truth. It is the origin or agent of cause. A principle is like a seed that has within its casing everything needed to reproduce itself, given the right conditions of soil and water. The advantage of communicating or teaching by principles is that the material is not age-specific, and the Holy Spirit enlightens each learner at his individual learning threshold. With key words defined, the principle can be taught and applied to any area of life or discipline of study. God's Word is full of principles, eternal truths that have the capacity to renew our minds and transform our actions.

We pray that the principles within this primer will generate a fresh vision of biblical family for each reader. May the light of God's Word and the fire of the Holy Spirit empower you to receive and engage truth in your marriage and family life. Put on the whole armor of God. Take up the sword of the Spirit. Discern and cast down every idol and stronghold in your culture. Return to the ancient pathways of the Lord, and restore wholeness and health to your home, your community, and your nation.

All thy children shall be taught of the Lord;
And great shall be the peace of thy children. (Isaiah 54:13 KJV)

ELIZABETH L. YOUMANS

CHAPTER 1

MARRIAGE, FAMILY, AND WORLDVIEW

This book examines the intertwined topics of marriage, family, and the rearing of children. We have all been profoundly shaped by a dense network of family relationships. Our very identity is found in the context of these relationships. I am not merely Scott, the individual. I am Scott, the husband of Kim; the father of Kaila, Jenna, Luke, Isaac, and Annelise; the son of Dale and Margaret; the brother of Craig and Susan; the grandson of Harry and Mabel; and so forth. You cannot rightly know me apart from these relationships. Furthermore, the very health and prosperity or the brokenness and dissolution of our nations are determined more by what is happening within these relationships than by just about any other factor. Given how important these relationships are, it is vital that we understand what the Bible teaches about them and let its truth be our sure foundation.

Yet for many of us, thinking biblically about marriage and family is something we've neglected to do. Because of the everyday familiarity of these relationships, there is a tendency to take them for granted. Our beliefs, values, and behaviors related to marriage and family rest upon a mountain of unexamined assumptions that we've absorbed from our parents, our friends, our teachers, the media, and the surrounding culture generally.

This is my story. I realized this early on in my married life when a non-Christian friend decided to "move in" with his girlfriend rather than marrying. Today, the practice of cohabiting has become commonplace in the United States and Europe. When I challenged the wisdom of his decision, my friend responded, "Why *should* I get married? Most of my married friends are now divorced. What's the point? Why not just live together and avoid the hassle and expense of a wedding, vows, and the legal headaches if we decide to separate?" As a Christian, I knew cohabiting was wrong but had no clear biblical response to his basic question.

So I began to think critically for the first time about these things: Why should people get married, as opposed to just living together? What is the *purpose* of marriage? What about children? What does the Bible say about children and the rearing of children? As I began to reflect, I realized my own thinking on these topics was influenced more by my culture than the Bible—but how could this be? I considered myself to be a committed Christian. Yet these topics weren't discussed much during my discipleship as a new Christian, nor did I recall hearing many sermons that addressed these basic questions. For that matter, I couldn't recall if these questions were covered in our premarital counseling! What I do recall were enjoyable, guided discussions aimed at better understanding the personality of my fiancée and practical ways we could build a harmonious husband-wife relationship. Nothing wrong with that, but the deeper questions were left unaddressed.

I've since come to see that this problem is much larger than I thought. We have a worldview crisis in the Church, and not only in my country. We have largely lost the biblical worldview for marriage and family, and as a result our understanding of these most basic and most important relationships is shaped more by the norms, customs, and values of our surrounding culture than by the Bible. As social beings, we are profoundly shaped by the culture we grow up in.

As Christians, however, we are called to think differently. We are called to inhabit the culture of God's kingdom and to think with "the mind of Christ" (2 Corinthians 2:16). We are called to "take every thought captive" (2 Corinthians 10:5) and "be transformed by the renewing of our minds." In short, we are called to think and act *differently*—not in accord with the accepted norms, attitudes, and behaviors of our surrounding culture, but in accordance with reality as presented in God's Word. This is nowhere more important than in how we think about the topics of marriage, family, and the raising of children.

Absolute truth exists and is sourced in God

A basic assumption behind this book is the concept of truth as being not relative but absolute, "existing independently of any other cause."[1] God, by His nature and in the creation, established order and the natural laws that govern life. The universe reflects God's orderly and sovereign rule. *"Yours, O Lord, is the greatness and the power and the glory and the victory and the majesty, for all that is in the heavens and in the earth is yours. Yours is the kingdom, O Lord, and you are exalted as head above all"* (1 Chronicles 29:11 ESV). The grand assumption, used alike by theologians, philosophers, and scientists, is that the world we experience every day is a cosmos—an ordered, harmonious whole—not a chaos. Creation has a rational structure that can, in part, be found by human reason.[2] *"That which is known about God is evident within them* [unrighteous men]; *for God made it evident to them. For since the creation of the world His invisible attributes, His eternal power and divine nature, have been clearly seen, being understood through what has been made, so that they are without excuse"* (Romans 1:19, 20).

God gave man the capacity to know truth and the responsibility to respond

Man, the crown of God's creation, is endowed with the unique ability to reason. God made the human mind and expects its virtuous application in life. Jesus said, *"You shall love the Lord your God with all your heart and with all your soul and with all your strength **and with all your mind**"* (Luke 10:27, emphasis added).

Man is to create culture from the creation God provided

We will elaborate further on this in chapter four, but here we would simply note the biblical

culture (n.) The sum total of ways of living built up by a group of human beings and transmitted from one generation to another.[3]

admonition in Genesis 1:28, "have dominion," as well as Genesis 2:15, *"The Lord God took the man and put him in the garden of Eden to work it and keep it."* Cultures do not materialize from nothing; they are the product of man's creativity. All the elements of human cultures—commerce, science, education, politics, the arts—spring from the mind of human beings created in God's image. In our fallen world, to one degree or another, the cultures we create either honor God or disobey His direction for human life.

Satan works through culture to enslave and destroy

Satan is a liar, and he uses lies to destroy lives and cultures. John 8:44 tell us that Satan *"was a murderer from the beginning, not holding to the truth, for there is no truth in him. When he lies, he speaks his native language, for he is a liar and the father of lies."* He uses lies to deceive and destroy, not only individuals but also entire nations. In Revelation 20:3, we read that at the end of time Satan will be thrown into the abyss in order to prevent his deceiving the *nations* any longer.

Satan deceives nations by working through the foundational worldview assumptions that shape a culture. In the New Testament, these deceptive worldview assumptions are referred to as "the basic principles of this world" that stand in contrast to the Truth of God's Word. In Colossians 2:20, the Apostle Paul admonishes followers of Christ, *"Since you died with Christ to the basic principles of this world, why, as though you still belonged to it, do you* [continue to] *submit to its rules?"* In a similar passage, Galatians 4:9, Paul says, *"But now that you know God—or rather are known by God—how is it that you are turning back to those weak and miserable principles? Do you wish to be enslaved by them all over again?"* In both passages, Paul uses the phrase "basic principles" to refer to these deceptive worldview assumptions that Satan uses to enslave both individuals and nations. Satan works through these elementary principles of culture to enslave and destroy. All nations—all cultures—can be likened to a tree. The tree will be healthy and fruitful when it is planted in the rich soil of God's truth. Yet Satan does his work of destroying nations by replacing the truth with lies at the level of the soil. The more truth that exists in the soil, the healthier the nation is. The more lies, the weaker the nation becomes, and if the lies become too great the nation will die.

GROWING HEALTHY CULTURES

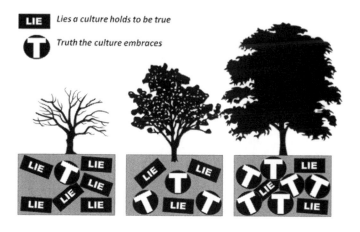

LIE *Lies a culture holds to be true*

T *Truth the culture embraces*

PRINCIPLE 1:
Our worldview establishes our beliefs, values, and behaviors

Everyone has a more or less coherent worldview that helps them understand and make sense of things. Our worldview is the sum total of the assumptions that we hold, whether consciously or unconsciously, that shape our view of reality. These assumptions are accumulated from our earliest days, implanted by our parents, siblings, and later by friends, teachers, media (books, television, etc.), and the institutions of our society—whether educational, economic, religious, or political. They function as lenses through which we see the world in a similar way to eyeglasses shaping the way we see things. They don't change the object in view, but they do change how we see it. In the words of law professor Phillip Johnson,

> **worldview** (n.) Translated from the German *Weltanschauung*, a comprehensive conception or image of the universe and of humanity's relation to it.[4]

> Understanding worldview is a bit like trying to see the lens of one's own eye. We do not ordinarily see our own worldview, but we see everything else by looking through it. Put simply, our worldview is the window by which we view the world, and decide, often subconsciously, what is real and important, or unreal and unimportant. . . . Our worldview governs our thinking even when—or especially when—we are unaware of it.[5]

As Professor Johnson makes clear, our worldviews are very important; indeed, they may be the *most* important, most consequential
thing about us because they wield power over our lives. They "govern our thinking" even when we are unaware of it.

biblical worldview The
worldview that comports
with Scripture, i.e., that rec-
ognizes God's claims over
the creation and over man.

Not only this, they determine what we value and,
ultimately, what we do—how we behave. They are
important because they provide us with answers to
the "big questions," including those dealing with
marriage and family: Should I get married? What is
the purpose of marriage? Should we have children? If so, how many,
and how should we raise them?

Applying this principle in your life

Ask God to bring your worldview into conformity with His Word as
you read and work through this book. While this book deals with
worldview only as it relates to family, excellent programs and resources are available to Christians who want to make sure their worldview in general is biblical. (See resources at the end of this chapter.)
Most Christians are surprised that some of their views are contrary to
Scripture. All of us can more fully develop a biblical worldview.

PRINCIPLE 2:
The dominant worldview of a community forms its culture

Worldviews affect individuals, but they also function collectively. In
any given community (or society or nation), there is a *dominant* worldview, which is established, upheld, and reinforced by the thought
leaders in a society—particularly those influential leaders in religion,
academia, government, and media. These thought leaders function
as cultural "gatekeepers" who use their positions of influence to rein-
force certain ideas, beliefs, values, and norms, and to exclude others.
For example, in the United States, while the majority of people would
identify themselves as Christians, the culture has become secularized. This has happened because, over the years, the influential elites
and the cultural gatekeepers largely adhere to a secular, materialistic
worldview. Once the worldview assumptions of the elites are "insti-
tutionalized," they influence virtually everyone within the society. All
of us are shaped far more deeply by our surrounding cultures than

we may realize. If you've had the experience of living for an extended time in a foreign country, you know just what I mean.

DOMINANT WORLDVIEW IMPACTS CULTURE

Applying this principle in your life

Write down three ways in which your beliefs as a Christian differ from the prevailing beliefs of the nation in which you live. Ask God to help you discern areas in which your own worldview has been learned from your culture rather than from the Bible.

PRINCIPLE 3:
Sexism destroys marriage and family

The lie of sexism is simply this: men are superior to women, or men are more valuable than women. Satan has woven this "basic principle of the world" into the social fabric of almost every nation, with devastating results. When this lie takes root within a culture, it shapes its institutions, including marriage and family. When husbands believe they are superior to their wives and daughters, they exercise authority as raw power. Women are treated as property—little more than slaves. It is no exaggeration to claim that this lie may be the single greatest source of poverty in our world today.

At a conference in Rwanda on the topic of men's attitudes toward women, one participant proclaimed without shame that "real men beat their wives." A Korean cultural proverb says that "dried fish and women are both better after they are beaten." In Pakistan, 70 to 90 percent of women have been physically abused by their husbands. Worldwide, 25 to 50 percent of women are victims of domestic violence, and one in seven will be raped in her lifetime. Another 2.5 million females every year are forced into sexual slavery. In the United States, the pornography industry has an annual revenue rate of approximately $12 billon—more than the annual revenue of all professional sports combined! In India, between two and five million female babies are aborted each year. One Indian abortion clinic advertises, "It is better to spend $38 now to terminate a female fetus than $3,800 later on her dowry." Researchers estimate at 100 million the number of women who have gone "missing" in the world. They are the victims of domestic violence and sex-selection abortions. What is at the root of this massive destruction? A lie woven by Satan into the very basic fabric of the culture: men are more valuable, more important, and superior to women.

Applying this principle in your life

Ask God to expose areas of your own heart in which the lie of sexism has found a place. This lie has brainwashed both men and women. God's Word and Spirit can set us free when we genuinely seek to know the truth; when we repent for believing the lie; and from our destructive attitudes, words, and actions based on sexism.

PRINCIPLE 4:
Secularism destroys marriage and family

At the core of secularism is the belief that knowledge is derived exclusively through what is perceived by the senses—what we see, hear, touch, taste, and feel. In other words, knowledge comes only through scientific inquiry. Because science is concerned with the material or physical realm, it cannot explain nonphysical or spiritual reality. The "lie" of secularism is that God and morality are not merely beyond the scope of scientific study but are actually unreal and illusory. For those in the grip of a secular worldview, the spiritual realm doesn't actually exist. There is no God in the heavens, and there is no soul or spirit within man. If God doesn't exist, and if man has no soul—if we are merely products of a purposeless process of evolution—then our lives have no purpose, and morality loses its foundation. There is no longer right or wrong, good or evil in any ultimate sense. If people choose to pretend that a "God" exists to help them cope with the uncertainties of life, that is their choice, but these personal, subjective choices have no standing in the public arena of government, law, business, or education.

Secularism has roots in ancient Greece and Rome, but modern secularism "came of age" during the European Enlightenment of the eighteenth century, a period when the modern scientific method was perfected with remarkable results. Great mysteries of the inner workings of the universe were being solved with breathtaking speed. As a result, a belief began to emerge: through science and reason alone, man could understand the cosmos. There was no need to appeal to God, divine revelation, or the authority of the Church. To Enlightenment thinkers, these outdated notions were holdovers from the previous "Dark Ages" of superstition, intolerance, and religious warfare. Today, secularism has become what author Nancy Pearcey calls "the dominant ideology of our day."[6] It is promulgated by urban elites who hold positions of influence in key cultural institutions. As such, they provide the "official" definitions of reality. In short, they serve as society's gatekeepers and are in a position to impose a secular worldview across an entire society.[7]

Satan uses the lie at the core of secularism to destroy marriages and families. If God doesn't exist, marriage is merely a manmade institution with no ultimate purpose beyond what people assign to it. We are free to "re-make it" as we want, or even to discard it altogether. And re-making and discarding traditional marriage is exactly what is happening in the West. Same-sex marriage is now recognized as legal in several European nations, Canada, and parts of the United States. Over 50 percent of marriages end in divorce in the United States and over 65 percent in Russia. Because of secularism and the sexual revolution that grew from its soil, sex has been decoupled from marriage and from reproduction. Sex, like marriage, loses any sense of purpose or meaning beyond personal gratification. It becomes little more than a spectator sport.

Today, throughout the secularized West, young people are opting out of marriage altogether. According to recent data from the Pew Research

Center, "The share of 30- to 44-year-olds living as unmarried couples has more than doubled since the mid-1990s."[8] This corresponds to another troubling number: in 2011, 51 percent of adults in the U.S. were married. This is the all-time lowest marriage rate recorded in the U.S.[9] In 1960, just over two-thirds (68 percent) of U.S. adults in their twenties were married. By 2008, that figure had dwindled to 26 percent.[10]

These are troubling developments. Social research tells us that cohabiting couples are less likely than married couples to stay together. They are more likely to experience assault, depression, and abortion. And the children of unmarried couples suffer proportionately. Not only does secularism destroy marriage, it also destroys the family. A stable population requires a fertility rate of 2.1 births per woman. When the birthrate of a society drops below 1.3, it becomes impossible to recover—the society basically goes extinct. Because of the breakdown in marriages throughout the secularized West, this tragedy is playing itself out before our eyes. Greece has a fertility rate of 1.3. Italy's is 1.2. Spain's is 1.1. These nations are on course to literally die out, and sooner than we might expect. Satan lurks behind this destruction. He lies at the level of foundational cultural beliefs, and his lies have penetrated the fabric of the culture and its institutions, with tragic consequences.

Applying this principle in your life

Do you believe that God's Word is absolute truth and that you are to live in conformity to His Word even if the world around you does not? Ask God to show you where you may have been influenced by the world's attitude toward marriage, divorce, sexual intimacy, and children. Repent where you see that your thinking and values have become compromised and weakened by the norms of society.

Closing Thoughts

We must recognize that we are in a spiritual battle at the level of basic cultural beliefs. Our weapon is the truth of God's Word, but we must develop the habit and discipline of thinking about all things biblically. One of Satan's most powerful lies has been to divide reality into two categories, sacred and secular. Christians who think in terms of the sacred and the secular tend to apply the teaching of the Bible solely to what are thought to be sacred or spiritual topics. These include God, religion, church, salvation, and personal holiness. Everything else is seen as secular, including politics, business, economics, the arts, and even marriage and family. Since these things are seen as secular, Christians mistakenly take their cues from the surrounding culture and its accepted norms and practices ("the basic principles of this world") in terms of how they think about such things.

The tragic result is that often Christians think and behave no differently from their surrounding culture. We must repent from this unbiblical way of thinking. We must resist dividing life into sacred and secular categories. God is the Lord of all, not just of some limited spiritual sphere. His truth applies to all areas of public life. To repent literally means to "change your mind." We must change our minds, replacing the unbiblical, sacred-secular way of thinking with a mindset that acknowledges the Lordship of Christ over every area and every topic, and that sees God's Word as the handbook for all areas of life, including marriage, family, and the raising of children.

Here's a suggested prayer you may want to use as you contemplate what you have read above and its application in your life.

Dear Father, thank You for the confidence we can have in life because of Your powerful truth. Forgive us for all the ways we have neglected to draw on Your wisdom as our guide. Forgive us where we have listened to Satan's lies, where we have yielded to the world the responsibility You gave us to create godly culture. By your Spirit's work, enable us to be faithful and fruitful in the task of creating cultures that honor You and Your Word. Amen.

Additional Resources

Miller, Darrow L., and Stan Guthrie. *Discipling Nations: The Power of Truth for Cultural Transformation*. Seattle, Wash.: YWAM Publishing, 2001.

Allen, Scott, Darrow Miller, and Bob Moffitt. *The Worldview of the Kingdom of God*. Seattle, Wash.: YWAM Publishing, 2001.

Pearcey, Nancy. *Total Truth: Liberating Christianity from its Cultural Captivity*. Wheaton, Ill.: Crossway, 2008.

Allen, Scott. *Beyond the Sacred-Secular Divide: A Call to a Wholistic Life and Ministry*. Seattle, Wash.: YWAM Publishing, 2011.

CHAPTER 2

PURSUING GOD'S DESIGN
FOR MARRIAGE

What is marriage? How do you define it? Marriage is the most ancient, most basic, and most foundational social unit in any nation. It is the foundation upon which families are built—upon which children are brought into the world and within which their character is formed, for better or worse. We live in a time when traditionally held ideas of marriage are being challenged as never before. Words matter, for they form the basic building blocks of a culture, and the word *marriage* has been fundamentally redefined over the past century. The *Encarta English Dictionary*—possibly the most referenced English dictionary in the world today—defines marriage this way: "A legally recognized relationship, established by a civil or religious ceremony, between two people who intend to live together as sexual and domestic partners."[11]

Now, compare this to the definition in Noah Webster's 1828 *American Dictionary of the English Language*:

The act of uniting a man and woman for life; wedlock; the legal union of a man and woman for life. Marriage is a contract both civil and religious, by which the parties engage to live together in mutual affection and fidelity, till death shall separate them. Marriage was instituted by God himself for the purpose of preventing the promiscuous intercourse of the sexes, for promoting domestic felicity, and for securing the maintenance and education of children.[12]

Take a moment to reflect on the dramatic differences between these two definitions. Today, marriage has been radically secularized—stripped of its God-given meaning. The breakdown in marriage we are witnessing today is the inevitable consequence.

- Webster's 1828 dictionary defines marriage as specifically between a man and a woman. The Encarta definition changes this to a relationship between "two people."

- Webster defines marriage as a "contract" for life. There is no mention of lifelong commitment in Encarta.

- Webster explicitly claims that marriage "was instituted by God." Encarta doesn't mention God at all, leaving the impression that marriage is a manmade institution and, thus, something man can freely re-create.

- Webster lists "the preventing of the promiscuous intercourse of the sexes" as a key purpose of marriage. This idea is completely missing in Encarta.

- Webster lists as a principle purpose of marriage "securing the maintenance and education of children." Encarta doesn't mention children at all, much less their care and education.

As followers of Christ, how should we respond to the dissolution of marriage? What will *we* do? Many of us are personally affected by the breakdown of marriage. We may be children of divorced parents—or we may be divorced ourselves. We may have done things that have deeply wounded our spouse or children. We may have aborted one or more children. A growing number of young people have never seen a positive example of a healthy, biblical marriage. As Christians, we must acknowledge our role in this brokenness. Rather than loving others as Jesus commanded (John 15:12), we have sinned against God, and harmed those we are closest to—our own husbands, wives, parents, children, or siblings. Too often we have not understood and, therefore, not obeyed God's clear design and instruction for marriage.

But thanks be to God, forgiveness is available through Christ. *"If we confess our sins, He is faithful and just to forgive us our sins and to cleanse us from all unrighteousness"* (1 John 1:9). Are there sins you need to confess to God and to those you have harmed? God is wonderfully gracious. He promises to wipe away our sins as far as east is from west (Psalm 103:12), but first we must humbly acknowledge the things we have done personally to harm marriage and family. We must follow the example of Israel's king David, who, after committing adultery with Bathsheba and arranging for the murder of her husband, confessed: *"Against you, you only have I sinned and done what is evil in your sight"* (Psalm 51:4).

Once we have confessed our own sin and failures, we face a choice. Will we be swept along by destructive cultural currents, or will we choose to follow God's way? Our prayer is that you will choose to follow God. If you do, then begin as Joshua did, with this solemn commitment: *"As for me and my house, we will serve the Lord"* (Joshua 24:15). All of us are either married, will be married, or know people who are married. We need to know God's way in marriage and family and consciously choose it. Perhaps more than at any other time in history, marriage cannot be taken for granted. A biblical marriage does not happen automatically. It must be pursued. So choose this day!

Marriage is ordained by God

The first thing we must say about marriage is that it is God's idea. It is His doing, and He defines it. God established marriage at the beginning of the world.

> *Then God said, "Let us make man in our image, after our likeness. And let them have dominion over the fish of the sea and over the birds of the heavens and over the livestock and over all the earth and over every creeping thing that creeps on the earth." So God created man in his own image, in the image of God he created him; male and female he created them. And God blessed them. And God*

said to them, "Be fruitful and multiply and fill the earth." (Genesis 1:26–28 ESV)

Marriage is addressed by several New Testament writers as well, especially Peter (1 Peter 3:1–8) and Paul (Ephesians 5:22–33; Colossians 3:18–19).

Marriage is the first and most basic social institution God created! Not incidentally, it is the only social institution created *before* the Fall. When we, intentionally or unintentionally, subscribe to any other idea of marriage than the one God defines, the consequences will *inevitably* be destructive. As missionary-statesman E. Stanley Jones wrote, "The moral laws are deeply embedded in the constitution of things—we do not break them, we break ourselves upon them."[13] Because God created marriage, it is inviolable—it is *sacred.* We are not free to redefine it without damaging ourselves and others.

Marriage is patterned after relationships in the Trinity

In Genesis 1:26–27 we read, *"Then God said, 'Let us make man in our image, in our likeness. . . .' So God created man in His own image, in the image of God he created him; male and female he created them."* Notice the plural "us" and "our" in reference to God. The Bible reveals God as "Trinity," that is, three persons: Father, Son, and Holy Spirit. This idea of three persons and one God is difficult to understand, yet it is one of the most basic and important doctrines of the Christian faith.

Before creation, a loving, other-serving relationship existed among God the Father, Son, and Holy Spirit. While on Earth, Jesus prayed to the Father in this way: *"You loved me **before the foundation of the world**"* (John 17:24, emphasis added). Before time and creation, a community of loving relationship existed within the godhead. Our deepest human longings—to love and to be loved—are rooted in the eternal existence and loving relationship within the Trinity, the God in whose image we are made. Because God is Triune, He decrees that man's solitude is "not good"—for Adam alone could never have reflected God's image. So God Himself "sets out to complete one of the central designs of creation, namely man and woman in marriage."[14] God created marriage to reflect (or to "image"), on a human

Trinity (n.) The one true God existing as three persons—Father, Son, and Holy Spirit—one in essence yet distinguished by their personal properties.

level, the relationship within the godhead. Husband and wife, joined in a loving, other-serving, one-flesh union, reflect something of the very nature of God.

Marriage is a "one-flesh" union between husband and wife

In Genesis 2:18–24, we read about the first marriage in history:

> *The Lord God said, "It is not good for the man to be alone. I will make a helper suitable for him." Now the Lord God had formed out of the ground all the beasts of the field and all the birds of the air. He brought them to the man to see what he would name them; and whatever the man called each living creature, that was its name. . . . But for Adam no suitable helper was found. So the Lord God caused the man to fall into a deep sleep; and while he was sleeping, he took one of the man's ribs and closed up the place with flesh. Then the Lord God made a woman from the rib he had taken out of the man, and he brought her to the man. The man said, "This is now bone of my bones and flesh of my flesh; she shall be called 'woman' for she was taken out of man." For this reason a man will leave his father and mother and be united to his wife, and they will become one flesh.* (Genesis 2:18–24)

husband (n.) A man contracted or joined to a woman by marriage.

wife (n.) A woman who is united to man in the lawful bonds of wedlock; the correlative of husband.

Here we see that marriage is the exclusive uniting of a man and a woman. Not a man and *a man*, a woman and *a woman*, a man and *an animal*, or a man and *multiple women*. Adam and Eve, as the first couple, whose relationship was established by God in the garden of Eden prior to the Fall, provide the model and pattern for all marriages that follow. Because God created Adam and Eve male and female, homosexuality (or so-called "homosexual marriage") is excluded.[15] Likewise, because Adam "could find no helper suitable" for himself among the animals, bestiality is excluded. Because God created just one woman for Adam, polygamy is excluded and the pattern of monogamy is established.[16] In Mark, Jesus affirms and amplifies Genesis 2:18–24:

> *"At the beginning of creation, God made them **male and female**. For this reason a man will leave his father and mother and be united to his wife, and the two will become one flesh. So they are*

no longer two, but one. Therefore, what God has joined together, let man not separate." (Mark 10:6-9, emphasis added)

Here again, we see that *marriage is God's doing*. It is He who creates, ordains, and performs this "one flesh" uniting. Jesus says explicitly that *"God* has joined" together husband and wife. Far from being merely a "legally recognized relationship between two people," marriage is a mysterious, lifelong uniting, *by God,* of a man and his wife. A pastor or priest may perform a wedding ceremony, but it is God who unites the husband and wife. In marriage, whatever one spouse does automatically includes the spirit of the other spouse and has an influence on him or her. The Apostle Paul puts it this way: in marriage, *"the wife's body does not belong to her alone but also to her husband. In the same way, the husband's body does not belong to him alone but also to his wife"* (1 Corinthians 7:3-4).

Marriage is a covenant intended to reflect God's covenant with His people

Marriage involves a solemn vow or covenant between husband and wife. This too reflects God's nature, for He is a covenant-making, covenant-keeping God. In the Old Testament, God makes a covenant with His chosen people Israel: *"I will take you to be my people, and I will be your God"* (Exodus 6:7, see also Exodus 29:45 and Leviticus 26:12). This covenant is extended to the Church—you and me— through Christ (Ephesians 2:11-22). This is the *"new covenant in my blood"* that Christ proclaimed in Luke 22:20. The Apostle Paul, in Ephesians 5:31-32, makes the astounding claim that marriage was created by God to be a reflection of this New Covenant between Christ and his bride, the Church:

> *For this reason a man will leave his father and mother and be united to his wife, and the two will become one flesh.* **This is a profound mystery—but I am talking about Christ and the church.** (emphasis added)

According to Pastor John Piper, "The most ultimate purpose of marriage is to put the covenant relationship of Christ and his church on display . . . a covenant-keeping love that reached its climax in the death of Christ for his church, his bride."[18] He goes on to say, "leaving parents and holding fast to a wife (or husband), and forming a new one-flesh union, is meant from the beginning to display the New Covenant—Christ's leaving his heavenly Father and taking the church as His bride, at the cost of his life, and holding fast to her in a one-spirit union forever."[19]

Understanding that marriages—all marriages—are intended by God to reflect the relationship between Christ and his bride is the *key* that unlocks the mystery of marriage. To grasp it is to understand why Paul admonishes husbands to *"love your wives as Christ loved the church and gave Himself up for her"* (Ephesians 5:25). This helps us understand Ephesians 5:23: *"For the husband is the head of the wife even as Christ is the head of the church."* It helps us understand why marrying a fellow believer is commanded in Scripture,[20] for it is impossible for husband and wife to pursue this deepest meaning of marriage when one of them does not accept it. In reflecting on this, Pastor Douglas Wilson draws some sobering conclusions:

> **covenant** (n.) A compact or agreement between two parties binding them mutually to undertakings on each other's behalf; a gracious undertaking entered into by God for the benefit and blessing of humanity.[17]

> A husband must always remember that as a husband he is a living picture of the Lord Jesus. This remembrance is his first duty in marriage. Since, as a husband, a man is speaking constantly about the Lord's relationship to His people, he ought to speak truthfully as well. The way a man treats his wife will determine whether he is speaking the truth about Christ or not.[21]

PRINCIPLE 1:
God hates divorce

Because God created the marriage relationship to reflect His covenant love to the Church, divorce is presented in Scripture as an abomination. It not only involves covenant breaking to the spouse, but more importantly, it involves telling a lie about Christ. He will *never* leave his wife.[22] Today, many couples justify divorce by saying, "I just don't love him (or her) anymore." But according to John Piper, "Marriage is not mainly about staying in love. It is about telling the truth with our lives. It is about portraying something true about Jesus Christ and the way he relates to His people."23 Our covenant-making, covenant-keeping God hates divorce (Malachi 2:16). When questioned about divorce, Jesus said, *"What God has brought together, let not man separate"* (Matthew 10:6). The terrible destruction and devastation wrought by divorce is a testament to the fact that marriage, unlike any other relationship, is uniquely "brought together" by God. The fact that the rates of divorce within the Church are identical to the rates outside the Church24 should drive us to our knees to cry out to God for mercy.

Applying this principle in your life

Read about Jesus' teachings on marriage and divorce (Matthew 5:31–32; 19:3–12; Luke 16:18). Also read Paul's teaching on the Christian and divorce (1 Corinthians 7:10–16). Ask forgiveness if any of these Scriptures apply to you. If your marriage is struggling, seek help from a couple in your church your pastor recommends. Meet weekly with that couple as they walk you through biblical principles of marriage and share from their own lives. In the United States, Marriage Savers is a ministry that trains couples to counsel other couples and claims a 90 percent reconciliation rate.[25] Marriage Ministries International is a ministry of couples in over 90 nations who teach and coach other couples in their homes.[26]

PRINCIPLE 2:
Sex was created exclusively for the marriage relationship

God designed sexual intercourse. He made it intensely pleasurable. It is a wonderful gift to be enjoyed, but it was created specifically for the marriage relationship. Sexual immorality—sex outside the life-long commitment of marriage—is consistently and repeatedly condemned throughout the Scripture. Illicit sex leads to great evil for any number of reasons, but particularly because of the link between sex and procreation. Marriage serves to prevent women from being exploited by men who might otherwise enjoy a sexual relationship for a time and then abandon the woman and any child she may have borne from that union.[27]

With the relatively recent development of increasingly effective means of birth control, sex has effectively been decoupled from both marriage and procreation. This, in turn, has given new license to everything from adultery to premarital sex and cohabiting—the rates of which are all skyrocketing. Many of the children produced through these unbiblical unions fall victim to abortion. The sexual revolution promised freedom and happiness; however, it has left in its wake a scorched landscape of diseased and destroyed lives, broken marriages and dying cultures—exactly the opposite of what God intends. This brings us to the fourth and final purpose for marriage: the promotion of domestic felicity—happiness!

Applying this principle in your life

Read about God's view of sex outside marriage (Exodus 2:14; 1 Corinthians 7:2; 5:1; 6:9–18; Galatians 5:19; Colossians 3:5; 1 Thessalonians 4:3). If you have been unfaithful to your spouse, ask God and your spouse to forgive you (Hebrews 13:4). Guard against entertainment that includes any form of pornography or endorses extramarital sexual activity. If necessary, get pastoral ministry for deliverance and healing to remain sexually pure.

PRINCIPLE 3:
God designed marriage to be a source of profound happiness

Our good God designed marriage to be a source of profound happiness, pleasure, and deep contentment—a life-giving, joy-filled adventure, not only for husband and wife but also for their children and extended family. Jesus said, *"The thief comes only to steal and kill and destroy. I came that they may have life and have it abundantly"* (John 10:10). Enjoying abundant life in marriage comes when we understand and pursue God's design and purposes for it. Not surprisingly, a growing body of research affirms this.

- Married men and women report less depression, less anxiety, and lower levels of other types of psychological distress than do those who are single, divorced, or widowed.

- One survey of 14,000 adults over a ten-year period found

that marital status was one of the most important predictors of happiness.

- When people married, their mental health improved—consistently and substantially.

- Studies have found that marriage improves emotional wellbeing in part by giving people a sense that their life has meaning and purpose.[28]

- God created marriage for our good. So it is no surprise that good fruit is the natural consequence. I certainly affirm this from my own experience.

Applying this principle in your life

Make a list of the ways in which your marriage brings joy, pleasure, and life to you, as well as of the ways in which you would like to have more contentment and fulfillment in marriage. Exchange your list with your spouse. Ask each other for suggestions. Meet with a couple who have been happily married for a long time and get ideas from them. Ask God to bring forth from your marriage the fullness of blessing that He intended.

Closing Thoughts

If you are married or desire to be married one day, I hope that these truths have deepened and elevated your vision for what marriage is as profoundly as they have mine! In the next chapter, we will explore family as a unit of government and consider more deeply the specific roles, duties, and responsibilities of husbands and fathers and of wives and mothers, as well as of children and the extended family, as provided in the Bible. There is no higher calling than to pursue a God-honoring marriage and the multiplication and discipling of godly offspring.

> Thank God for your marriage. Ask him to establish it, to confirm it, to sanctify it, and preserve it, so your marriage will be 'for the praise of his glory. Amen.' (Dietrich Bonheoffer, *Letters and Papers from Prison*)[29]

Here is a suggested prayer:

Dear Father, thank You for inventing this powerful human relationship called marriage. We are enriched as humans by this gift. Yet we must confess that we have neglected and even abandoned Your sacred definition of marriage. Our societies have seen fit to "redefine" marriage. Even in our churches we have often failed to clearly uphold the sanctity of marriage. Create in us a clean heart for Your eternal principles of one-man, one-woman marriage. Strengthen our marriages. In Your Church, establish the pattern of marriage that will honor You and restore biblical standards in our land. Amen.

Additional Resources

Keller, Timothy. *The Meaning of Marriage: Facing the Complexity of Commitment with the Wisdom of God*. New York: Dutton Adult, 2011.

Wilson, Douglas. *Reforming Marriage*. Moscow, Idaho: Canon Press, 2012.

Piper, John. *This Momentary Marriage: A Parable of Permanence*. Wheaton, Ill.: Crossway, 2012.

CHAPTER 3

GOD'S DESIGN FOR THE FAMILY

The family is the oldest and most basic of human institutions.[30] It is "the original society in which each person is placed by God at birth," writes pastor and author Philip Lancaster. "It is, for better or worse, the place where people are shaped—their intellect, their values, their character, and their aspirations. All that a person later becomes depends upon the factors that forged him in his youth, and the home is the primary shaper of young human beings."[31]

In this chapter, we'll look at the basic pattern of family life presented in Scripture, along with the specific roles of the husband, father, wife, mother, and children. God has graciously provided a wealth of guidance and instruction in His Word for how we are to function as families. As we touch on some of the key biblical passages, our goal will be to provide the broad contours and framework for what a Christ-honoring family should look like.

God defines an authority structure for the family, with the husband as "head"

As a God-ordained institution, the family has a built-in authority structure. To put it simply, the husband is leader (or head) of the wife, and the parents are leaders of the children. God has granted the position of "head" to the husband, but what exactly does headship in the family mean? As we saw in chapter two, God created the institution of marriage to be a reflection of Christ's relationship to His bride, the Church.

authority (n.) The right to command or to act. Jesus indicates that authority in His kingdom is exercised in servanthood.

As Christ is the head of the Church, it follows that the husband is the head of the wife, as the Apostle Paul clearly states in Ephesians 5:23. By using this metaphor, Paul highlights the husband's special responsibility as his wife's leader and protector. Pastor John Piper offers this concise and helpful definition of headship: "Headship is the divine calling of a husband to take primary responsibility for Christ-like, servant leadership, protection and provision in the home."[32] In short, headship is not mainly a right or privilege but a burden and responsibility.

It is critical that husbands understand that they do not choose to be the head—they simply *are* the leaders, whether they want to be or not! In Ephesians 5:23, Paul does not say that husbands *ought* to be the heads of their wives. He says that they *are*. A man is not granted this position by God because he is in any way better than or superior to his wife; he is given it because that is God's arrangement for home government. Whatever happens in the family, the "buck stops" with the husband—God holds him accountable. His authority as head is a *delegated authority*; he is a steward acting on behalf of God, who is the true Lord of the home. This is seen in the fact that Adam was held responsible by God for the fall into sin, even though it was Eve who first ate from the tree. "*The Lord **called to the man** and said, 'where are you?'*" (Genesis 3:9, emphasis added). This is how governing authority works. The head answers for all those under his authority.[33]

Unfortunately, men from Adam onward have inherited an inclination for avoiding the demands of headship. If you are a husband and father, I urge you to embrace this high calling. As you assume this mantle of leadership, remember that you are not alone. Christ, our supreme leader, is with you. He is committed to your success and has promised to be your help. "*I can do all things through Christ who strengthens me*" (Philippians 4:13). Lean on Him.

God intends for those in authority to be responsible servants

Before creation, authority existed for all eternity within the godhead. The *head* of Christ is God (the Father). The Son *submits* to the Father

(Luke 22:42; John 17:4), and the Holy Spirit *submits* to the Father and the Son (John 14:26; 15:26). In the Bible, authority structures exist to create order. If there is no order—if every person does what is right in his own eyes—there is chaos. Order is a prerequisite for freedom. One writer has called order "the first need of all."[34]

In God's kingdom, *all authority* is a form of sacrificial service rather than tyranny. Jesus upheld the concepts of authority and submission, while completely revolutionizing them. Here is how He taught His disciples to understand authority:

> *"You know that the rulers of the Gentiles lord it over them, and their great ones exercise authority over them.* **It shall not be so among you.** *But whoever would be great among you* [that is, in a position of authority] *must be your servant, and whoever would be first among you must be your slave,* **even as the Son of Man came not to be served, but to serve,** *and to give his life as a ransom for many."* (Matthew 20:25-27, emphasis added)

Jesus modeled this authority-as-servant teaching by washing the feet of His followers before going to the cross on their behalf. *"If I then, your Lord and teacher* [your authority], *have washed your feet, you ought to wash one another's feet"* (John 13:14). Servanthood doesn't nullify leadership in Scripture; it defines it.[35] Likewise, the concept of submission in Scripture does not imply inferiority. Jesus, the Son, was in no way inferior to God the Father. He said, *"I and the Father are one"* (John 10:30), yet He placed himself in submission to the Father (John 14:31). To follow God's way in marriage and family, it is critical that we understand family as a unit of government with a built-in authority structure. But it is equally critical that we understand the authority structure *biblically*.

Today, it is common for many to reject notions of headship and authority. In the West, an entire generation (those who matured during the 1960s and 70s) was defined by its willingness to "question authority." At one level, this is understandable, given the many examples of tyrannical authority in our broken world. Far too many men have used their authority to "lord it over" others, using power to manipulate and achieve selfish ends. If you struggle with the concepts of authority and submission, I urge you not to abandon them. Instead, consider them from a biblical perspective. Authority and submission are fundamental principles of reality and, when understood biblically, are necessary and positive, not only for families but also for healthy communities and nations.

The family functions as the most basic unit of government in any nation

When we think of "government," we tend to think in terms of politics and politicians, whether local, state or provincial, or national. Yet the family is actually the most basic form of government in any society. The role of the husband as "head" of the household is to be respected, not only by those within the family but by church and civil authorities as well.

When a man and woman leave the homes of their parents and join in the one-flesh union of marriage (Genesis 2:24), they lay the foundation for a new family with its own distinct authority structure. From this moment, the wife is no longer under the headship of her father but of her husband. Likewise, the husband is no longer under his father's authority but now assumes headship in relation to his wife. This is beautifully illustrated in most wedding ceremonies when the father of the bride places her hand into the hand of her new husband—her new head. It is essential that *both* husband and wife "leave" the authority of their parents when they join in marriage. While they continue to have a duty to honor their parents (Exodus 20:12) and even to provide for their needs when necessary (Mark 7:6–13), they are no longer under their governing authority. Unless these transfers of authority happen, conflict and confusion inevitably follow.

father (n.) He who begets a child. The obvious implication is that only a male can be a father.

While God created the family to be a basic unit of government, it is not the only one. The local church is another form of government, along with the state or civil government. Each of these forms of government has an indispensible function within the larger society. The family is the primary place where children are to be nurtured, educated, and equipped to be godly, self-governing citizens. When each form of government understands and fulfills its God-given function, while respecting the roles of the others, society flourishes.

PRINCIPLE 1:
The husband is to lovingly and sacrificially lead the family

According to Pastor Philip Lancaster, the husband "has the calling and position to be the primary molder of the family. He may abdicate his role or do a poor job, but that, too, shapes the family. There is no escaping his influence—for better or worse."[36] In our day, manhood is in retreat and fatherhood is a mystery to many men. In the West, the contemporary feminist movement has deeply distorted the biblical understanding of manhood. In other parts of the world, masculinity equates to "machismo," suggesting a controlling and oppressive tyrant. The recovery of biblical manhood as expressed in the roles of husband and father may be among the greatest needs in our world today. This recovery must begin by a careful study of God *the Father* and Christ *the Bridegroom* as our ultimate examples. The Father-heart of God is beautifully portrayed in Psalm 23, which illustrates what it means for husbands and fathers to "shepherd" their wives and children. Here we see God as leader (*"He leads me beside quiet waters. . . . He guides me in paths of righteousness"*), as the provider (*"I shall not want. . . . my cup overflows"*), as the spiritual shepherd (*"He restores my soul"*), and as the protector (*"Even though I walk through the valley of the shadow of death, I will fear no evil for You are with me"*).

Ephesians 5:25 says, *"Husbands, love your wives as Christ loved the church and gave himself up for her."* A man must love his wife *sacrificially*. This is his most fundamental duty. Far from being a mere feeling or emotion, love, as detailed in 1 Corinthians 13:4–7, must be *chosen*. Husbands are duty-bound to love their wives *as their own bodies, "for no one ever hated his own flesh, but nourishes and cherishes it"* (Ephesians 5:28–29). The word *cherish* means "to keep warm, to cherish with a tender love."[37] He is prohibited from coveting the wife of another man (Exodus 20:17) and commanded to *"rejoice in the wife of your youth"* and *"be enraptured with her love"* (Proverbs 5:15–23). Furthermore, husbands are to live with their wives in an understanding way, showing honor to the wife (1 Peter 3:7). She is due this dignity because God created her in His image. She must be the most important person in his life other than the Lord. She is his partner, his lover, his best counselor, his friend.[38] As such, every husband "is under the most solemn obligations to do all in his power to make his wife's life happy, beautiful, noble and blessed. To do this, he must be ready to make any personal sacrifice. Nothing less than this can be implied in loving as Christ loved the His church when he gave himself for it."[39]

The husband/father is also called to be the leader in the home. This leadership involves having a *vision* for his family, taking *initiative*, and *sustaining* that initiative. Our heavenly Father has a vision for us—that we would be conformed to the likeness of His Son (Romans 8:29). Furthermore, He takes the initiative to sanctify us and carries that process through to completion. Likewise, husbands are to have a vision for their families and *take initiative* in moving toward it. Leadership does not assume it is superior—instead, it takes initiative.[40] For example, if there is a conflict between husband and wife, leadership means that the husband takes the initiative in reconciliation, no matter who is at fault.

The husband's leadership in the home is critical for another reason. A man who has not learned to shepherd his own family has not developed the character necessary to exercise authority in other areas of life. Conversely, if he succeeds at home, he is prepared for success elsewhere. In 1 Timothy 3:5, Paul states that a man must prove his skill as a family shepherd before he is considered ready to be an elder in the church. Faithfulness in the smaller sphere of the home is necessary before a man can be entrusted with stewardship of a larger sphere (Matthew 25:21). Puritan pastor Hugo Grotius (1583–1645) said:

> He knows not how to rule a kingdom, that cannot manage a Province; nor can he wield a Province, that cannot order a City; nor he order a City, that knows not how to regulate a Village; nor he a Village, that cannot guide a Family; nor can that man Govern well a Family that knows not how to Govern himself; neither can any Govern himself unless his reason be Lord, Will and Appetite her Vassals; nor can Reason rule unless herself be ruled by God, and (wholly) obedient to Him.[41]

Applying this principle in your life

If you are a husband and a father, do you take consistent leadership in caring for your family and the issues that arise? Write down three areas in which you need to assume greater leadership. What areas of Christian self-government need to be strengthened in order for you to successfully shepherd your family? Write them down and ask the Lord to help you make a simple plan to address them.

household (n.) The Bible often uses the word "home" or "household" interchangeably with "family." In the Bible, a household consists of parents (husband and wife) and children, with or without relatives, friends, and servants in addition.

PRINCIPLE 2:
The husband is to protect and provide for his family

As the good Shepherd protects His flock, so the husband protects those in his household. Protection involves awareness of both spiritual and physical danger, initiative, and, often, courage. Imagine a couple is awakened by a noise and suspects a burglar. A husband doesn't say to his wife, "It's your turn to check it out. I went last time." Even if the wife has a black belt in karate, the husband is duty-bound to take the initiative and investigate the sound. She may finish the burglar off with a swift kick to the head, but the husband had better be lying unconscious on the floor, or he is no man![42] In the spiritual realm, the godly husband views sin, death, and hell as fearful enemies, and he commits himself to protecting his wife and children from them all. So he takes initiative in protecting those in his household from evil influences that may encroach through the television or internet. Protection means that he sometimes acts as a dispenser of discipline. Such discipline shows that a father is determined to protect his family from evil and its destructive consequences.[43]

In addition to protection, provision is at the heart of fatherhood. Paul says in 1 Timothy 5:8 that a man who does not provide for his household is worse than an unbeliever. Such negligence is the equivalent of apostasy—it is a denial of Christ, who feeds His bride. Our heavenly Father provides extravagantly for our needs, and so fathers and husbands provide for their households—indeed, husbands are "hardwired" by God to be providers. One of the most painful experiences a man can endure, when faced with unemployment or injury, is the inability to provide for his family even for a time.

The Bible requires a husband to supply his household with basic needs—food, shelter, and clothing (Exodus 21:10)—and to meet the sexual needs of his wife (1 Corinthians 7:3–4). The husband bears the *primary* responsibility to put food on the table. This does not mean there are no times when a wife can work outside the home or that the husband cannot share the domestic burdens. But it does mean that a man compromises his soul and sends the wrong message to his wife and children when he does not position himself as the one who lays down his life to provide for his family.[44]

The husband and father's role also involves being the spiritual provider for the household. He is to "pastor" his wife and children. The fourth commandment requires the father to lead his whole family in Sabbath-keeping (Exodus 20:8–11). Husbands and fathers should pray daily for their family in this way: "Lead them not into temptation but deliver them from evil" (Matthew 6:12, 13). Husbands should take the initiative to regularly gather wife and children for family devotions, times of prayer and Bible reading.[45]

Applying this principle in your life

If you are a husband and father, how would you assess yourself as a protector and provider of your family, both physically and spiritually? What are your strengths and weaknesses? What specific things can you commit to God to do to shore up the weak areas of protection and/or provision?

PRINCIPLE 3:
The wife is to respect and faithfully submit to her husband

A godly wife is truly priceless to her husband, family, community, and nation. Indeed, she is *"more precious than jewels"* (Proverbs 31:10). Her task is nothing less than that of helping her husband to build a strong and godly family and society. Both husband and wife are created by God in His image. They are coequals in terms of their value and dignity. While God is named "Father" in the Bible, note-worthy passages reveal God's "motherly" attributes. The Bible uses simile to compare God to a nurturing mother. God is like a woman giving birth (Isaiah 42:14; 46:3), a nursing mother (Isaiah 49:13–15; 66:10–13), a mother hen (Matthew 23:37; Luke 13:34), and a mother eagle (Exodus 19:4; Deuteronomy 32:10–12).[46]

The principle metaphor of marriage in Scripture, as we have stressed, is the relationship between Christ, the head, and the Church, the bride. In using this metaphor, the Apostle Paul highlights the husband's special responsibility as his wife's leader and protector, *and the wife's calling to accept her husband in that role*, just as the Church submits to the headship of Christ. This in no way implies that the wife is inferior. The two have equal dignity and value, and they are to fulfill their roles in marriage on the basis of a mutual respect that is rooted in this fact.[47]

Today, the word *submit* carries enormous negative connotations. Yet far from submission being a position of groveling inferiority, even Christ freely submits to the will of the Father (Luke 22:42). As followers of Christ, we are all to walk in submission to Him. The Apostle Paul admonishes the Church to *"submit to one another out of reverence for Christ"* (Ephesians 5:21). In marriage, Peter states, *"Wives, be subject to your own husbands"* (1 Peter 3:1). Women are not instructed to submit to all men, but only the wife to her own husband. Submission in marriage should be characterized by a *disposition* on the part of the wife to follow her husband's authority—an *inclination* to yield to his leadership. It is an attitude that says "I delight for you to take the initiative in our family. I am glad when you take responsibility and lead with love. I don't flourish in the relationship when you are passive, and I have to make sure the family works."[48] Submission does not mean that the wife puts the will of her husband before the will of Christ. The wife is a follower of Christ before and above being a follower of her husband.

If the most basic duty of a husband is to love his wife, then the most basic duty of a wife is to respect her husband (Ephesians 5:33). Of course, a wife must also love her husband (Titus 2:4). All believers are required to *"love their neighbors as themselves"* (Mark 12:33), but in the particular relationship of wife to husband, the emphasis is on respect. Christ loves His bride, the Church, and the Church respects the authority of Christ. The Bible encourages believers to honor and respect governing authorities (Romans 13:1–7; Titus 3:1; 1 Peter 2:13), and this holds true within the family. Such respect on the part of the wife entails honor, as well as an inclination to yield to her husband's leadership.[49] Of course, a husband should live so that he is worthy of his wife's respect. Yet even if he fails in his high calling, she should remember hers. Her respect for her husband affirms his leadership in the family and, as such, is a powerful source of encouragement to him.

Applying this principle in your life

If you are a wife, how inclined have you been to follow your husband's initiative and leadership? Would you say that you accept his leadership more readily when he agrees with you, or do you consistently accept, honor, and yield to the direction that he determines is best for the family? Perhaps you would like him to assume more leadership, or perhaps you believe he lacks wisdom in certain areas of family life. Regardless of his current maturity as the family shepherd, he will grow in leadership and love as you pray for him regularly, and as you trust God to prosper the whole family in following His appointed head. Write down several things you can do to become a more supportive and encouraging wife. Bless him in person and in prayer.

mother (n.) A female parent; especially, one of the human race; a woman who has borne a child; correlative to son or daughter.

PRINCIPLE 4:
The wife is to bear and nurture children and manage the household

The first command by God to mankind in Scripture is to *"be fruitful and multiply."* Here, the wife and mother plays a vital role—not only in bearing children but in tenderly nurturing them (1 Thessalonians 2:7). Her duty to love and nurture her children is essential to their healthy development. This invaluable role is something her body is uniquely designed for. Our sexually libertine societies often reduce women's breasts to sex objects; yet God, who designed the breast, is the God of nurture. He is comforting, nurturing, and providing (Isaiah 66:10–13).[50] The Hebrew word for breast is *shad*, the root of one of the names of God, *El Shaddai*, which means God Almighty. God is the one who provides His people with succor and nourishment, and it is the high calling of the mother to provide this same nurturing to her children.

Titus 2 and Proverbs 31 present a picture of the godly woman as an industrious and productive "home worker," whose calling is centered on her husband and children. In her domestic role, she complements her husband in his public role. In the secular, industrialized West, we are far removed from the image of the "household" as portrayed in Scripture or common in the United States through the early 1900s. Consequently, it is almost impossible to appreciate the incredible skills required of a wife and mother to govern her household. Today a "housewife" is often viewed negatively, both within and outside the Church. In earlier generations, the home was not only a basic unit of government; it also had vital economic, educational, and charitable functions. The godly wife portrayed in Proverbs 31 is busy with a variety of economic activities: *"She seeks wool and flax and works with willing hands. . . . She considers a field and buys it; with the fruit of her hand she plants a vineyard. . . . She perceives that her merchandise is profitable"* (vv. 13–18).

The industrial revolution displaced the home with the factory and corporation as centers of economic activity. Today husbands, and increasingly wives, *leave* the home to "go to work." Children are viewed as an economic expense rather than a valuable source of labor. Similarly, the educational role of the household has been displaced. Now children "go to school" and are educated primarily by people other than parents. Home-based charity has been displaced by government welfare programs. While well intentioned, many of these changes have had the effect of weakening family bonds. Now many elderly people, for example, look to the government, rather than their families, to provide for them in old age.

As these historic functions of the household have diminished, the institution of the family has weakened. When Titus 2:5 urges wives to be *"busy at home,"* many women today wonder what, exactly, they are supposed to be busy doing with the husband off at work and the kids at school. Accordingly, many women are *leaving* the home and entering the workforce in search of significance and extra income. While perhaps understandable, this departure only further weakens already fragile families. Today, many "homes" are little more than bedrooms—places for family members to sleep for a few hours before going their separate ways. Even such basic functions as preparing and enjoying meals together are being lost. God created the family to play a central role in the functioning of a healthy society. As its basic functions have been displaced, the fabric of society has weakened.

So how should we respond? I believe households thrive when these core functions—economic, educational, and charitable—are reclaimed, at least to some degree, and as the wife assumes leadership in the home, devoting energy to her husband and children. Does this mean women should never work outside the home? Not necessarily. There certainly may be seasons when a wife works outside the home. While there is no returning to the preindustrial era, nor should we desire this, there are choices that families can make to restore these essential functions. Such choices will almost always be countercultural, and therefore a source of resistance and controversy—yet such decisions are necessary if we are to pursue God's way in marriage. The primary responsibility for educating children is one area that many parents can take steps to reclaim. Another is restoring the household as a center of charity.

Applying this principle in your life

If you are a wife and mother, do you highly value your role as nurturer of your children and manager of your household? Or have you let the culture's devaluing of this God-ordained role rob you of joy and fulfillment? Examine your heart before the Lord, and ask Him to impart to you the high esteem in which He holds you in your role. Husbands, encourage your wives and praise them often for the work they do. Fathers, take leadership in educating your children and in supporting your wife's partnership with you in this role. Talk together and seek God for ways in which she can be more fully released to fulfill the role that God has ordained for her. Write down the ideas on which you agree.

PRINCIPLE 5:
Children are to honor and obey parents

Children also have specific duties in Scripture. The fifth commandment requires children to *"honor your father and your mother"* (Exodus 20:12). In Mark 7:6–13, Jesus fiercely opposed the Pharisees' brand of piety, which was actually an evasion of their responsibility to honor parents. His own last act before He died was to provide for His mother's future (John 19:25–27).[51] While they are under the authority of their father and mother, children are commanded to obey their parents (Ephesians 6:1; Colossians 3:20). As they grow up and marry, becoming authorities in their own households, they are no longer obligated to obey parents—but the requirement to honor their parents remains.

While children are required to obey parents, the parents must help their children fulfill this responsibility. Mothers and fathers who allow their children to willfully disobey are doing them no favors; rather, they are enabling their disobedience to God's direct command. This is why the Bible emphasizes the responsibility of parents to discipline their children,[52] and why such discipline is rightly called an act of love. *"Whoever spares the rod hates his son, but he who loves him is diligent to discipline him"* (Proverbs 13:24). *The purpose of godly discipline is always correction, never punishment.* Ephesians 6:4 says, *"Fathers, do not provoke your children to anger, but bring them up in the discipline and instruction of the Lord."* In order for the discipline not to provoke children to anger, it must not be excessive, and it must be fairly and consistently applied to all children without favoritism. It is not simple or easy for parents to correctly discipline their children, but that is no excuse for neglecting it.

Applying this principle in your life

What do you as a parent currently do in your family to encourage children to honor and obey you? Are you seeing the fruits of honor and obedience developing in them? Ask the Lord to show you areas of their lives that need more careful and consistent supervision, instruction, and correction. Consider asking for ideas from other Christian parents whose children demonstrate honor, respect, and cheerful obedience toward them.

Closing Thoughts

God is the creator of marriage, the designer of the family. When we understand His blueprint—when we function as husbands, fathers, wives, mothers, and children according to His design—we reap a bountiful harvest of joy, the kind that only strong, healthy families experience. If, however, we function in our family roles on the basis of unbiblical patterns, there will inevitably be negative, destructive consequences. Most of us take our cues from our parents or the broader culture when it comes to how we function in the family. As followers of Christ, this ought not to be. We must be intentional in our study of Holy Scripture as we seek to understand and obey God's clear instructions for the family. Our nations are being destroyed from within for lack of godly, Christ-honoring families. I pray that you will be part of the solution for your nation. Choose this day!

Dear Father, We praise You for the gift of family. We are renewed in our desire to grow in our understanding of Your principles of family, and to grow in our function as a family. We want our family to reflect Your design. Enable us by Your Holy Spirit to faithfully present to the society around us an example of a family that conforms to Your design. Forgive us for adopting the false and harmful models around us. Use us to build a nation of strong families that bring honor to Your name! Amen.

Additional Resources

Piper, John. *What's the Difference? Manhood and Womanhood Defined According to the Bible.* Wheaton, Ill.: Crossway, 2008.

Wilson, Nancy. *Praise Her in the Gates: The Calling of Christian Motherhood.* Moscow, Idaho: Canon Press, 2000.

Carlson, Allan C., and Paul T. Mero. *The Natural Family: A Manifesto.* Dallas, Tex.: Spence Publishing Company, 2007.

CHAPTER 4

GOD'S PURPOSE FOR THE FAMILY IN DISCIPLING NATIONS

What is God's ultimate aim in creation? Is it to see people from every nation come to a saving faith in Christ? Is it to see new churches planted? Is it to see the hungry fed? These are all important, but they are not God's ultimate aim. They should be viewed as essential "means," not ends. God's ultimate end is that the knowledge of His glory would fill the earth as the waters cover the seas (Habakkuk 2:14). To be sure, this ultimate purpose won't be fully realized until Christ returns. But until then, on the basis of His finished work on the cross, Jesus calls us to pray and to work in His strength to advance His kingdom "on earth as it is in heaven" (Matthew 6:10).

Not only does God have a comprehensive plan for creation, He has a strategy to advance it. It is an "inside-out" process of transformation that begins at the level of human hearts and minds. By the transforming power of the gospel, individuals are "born again" as "new creations" (John 3:3; 2 Corinthians 5:17) filled with the Spirit and enabled to do God's will. From here, transformation begins to

transformation (n.) Change in the nature of something, whether the heart and life of an individual, the life of a family, or the character and behavior of a nation.

ripple outward into the social sphere. The first, most basic and most important social sphere is that of the family. As husband and wife pursue God's way in marriage, they and their children are blessed. Such parents disciple their children to be the self-governing, "godly offspring" our Lord desires. They carefully prepare them to exercise godly dominion in every area of society. In due time, as these children assume positions of influence in the various spheres of society, these areas are reformed and increasingly reflect God's knowledge and righteousness. When this happens, the nation is blessed—the nation is *discipled*.

The local church and its leaders play an essential role in this process. They not only proclaim the good news of salvation in Christ but serve as "equipping centers" (Ephesians 4:2). They equip singles for marriage, parents to be the primary disciplers of their children, and members of the body to advance God's kingdom in every area of society. The Church also serves a prophetic role as the conscience of the nation.

THE INSIDE-OUT PROCESS OF DISCIPLING NATIONS

Vision: Hab. 2:14 → *Discipled Nations*

Spheres of Society*

Family

Character

Worldview

Spiritual Regeneration

* Government, arts, media, education, commerce, etc.

Two important points need to be made about this process. First, it doesn't happen overnight! You may see little progress in your lifetime. Things may get worse before they get better, because we face stiff opposition. Our enemy, Satan, is busily advancing his counterfeit kingdom. He is planting his weeds in the midst of the wheat of

God's kingdom, and the two grow side-by-side (Matthew 13:36–43). We can expect him to do everything in his power to oppose us, yet by the blood of Christ we can resist him as we put on the full armor of God described in Ephesians 6:10–18. Transformation is the work of God through *generations.* This is why the family is so central to God's plan, for it is a uniquely multi-generational institution. With the hearts of the children won to their father and their father's God, the cause of Christ in the world can go forward though the generations.[53]

Second, transformation at every level (individual, family, and nation) is contingent upon transformation in the preceding level. Another way of saying this is "as the family goes, so goes the nation." Theodore Cuyler affirms this:

> I care little for the government which presides at Washington, in comparison with the government which rules the millions of American homes. No administration can seriously harm us if our home life is . . . godly. No statesmanship or legislation can save us, if once our homes become the abode of profligacy. The home rules the nation.[54]

God created marriage and family to carry out the cultural mandate

God blessed Adam and Eve, the first couple. He placed them in a magnificent garden and gave them a task: "*Be fruitful and increase in number; fill the earth and subdue it. Rule over the fish of the sea and the birds of the air and over every living creature that moves on the ground*" (Genesis 1:28). This mandate is expanded upon in Genesis 2:15: "*The Lord God took the man and put him in the garden of Eden to work it and take care of it*" (emphasis added). These tasks are sometimes referred to as the cultural mandate. The garden of Eden perfectly displayed the knowledge and glory of God. It was perfect, but it wasn't complete. Adam and Eve and their offspring, as image-bearers of God, were to rule as kings and queens over God's magnificent creation on His behalf. They were to use their creativity and imagination to create God-glorifying *culture*, to develop new works of art, music, poetry, science, and technology. God's purpose was (and is) to fill the Earth with the

cultural mandate Sometimes called the "creation mandate," this term refers to God's command to the first human couple to tend the garden and cause the creation to be fruitful. All human activity toward the creation flows from this mandate.

knowledge of His glory (Habakkuk 2:14). Though the Fall damaged our ability to fulfill this mandate, the task remains, and marriage was designed specifically to carry it out.

PRINCIPLE 1:
Husbands and wives play essential, yet distinct, roles in carrying out the cultural mandate

In fulfilling this high calling, Adam required a companion, "*a **helper** suitable for him*" (Genesis 2:18, emphasis added). He needed a partner perfectly designed to complement and complete his strengths. The cultural mandate was given by God to *both* Adam and Eve, but they have different roles to play in carrying it out. These roles reflect the unique roles of the Father, Son, and Holy Spirit, both in creation and in redemption.[56] In other words, the unity and diversity of the Triune God extends to the human realm in marriage. Douglas Wilson describes the roles of husband and wife this way: "They need one another, but they need one another differently. The man needs the help; the woman needs to help. . . . He is called to the work and must receive help from her. She is called to the work through ministering to him. He is oriented to the task, and she is oriented to him."[57] Contrary to common understanding, there is no sense of inferiority in the word *helper*. In fact, in our daily experience, it is the strong who typically help the weak. God is often referred to in Scripture as our helper (Isaiah 41:10).

role (n) Proper or customary function.[55]

Today, many reject the God-given roles of husband and wife. The present-day feminist movement has blurred the distinctive roles and design of men and women. As a result, men are increasingly feminized, while women are encouraged to deny their feminine nature and act like men. There is a crying need in this generation to reclaim the distinctive biblical design and roles of husband and wife in fulfilling the cultural mandate.[58]

Applying this principle in your life

Talk with your spouse about your roles in marriage. Plan how together you can be even more compatible partners in cultivating a home and family full of the life of Christ. Discuss how each member can prosper and know abundant love and blessing, which can then overflow into the lives of others and their families. Seek God together in prayer for specific steps to take.

PRINCIPLE 2:
Marriage exists to produce godly offspring

The cultural mandate of Genesis 1:28 begins with the *first* command given by God in Scripture: *"Be fruitful and increase in number; fill the earth."* It is repeated to Noah and his sons after the flood in Genesis 9:1. Malachi 2:15 makes God's intentions plain: *"Did* [God] *not make* [husband and wife] *one, with a portion of the Spirit in their union? And what was God seeking?* **Godly offspring"** (emphasis added). Simply put, God created marriage for the purpose of multiplying godly offspring—reflectors of His image and glory—across the face of the Earth. On a human level, there is nothing more miraculous than God's partnership with husband and wife in the creation of an entirely new human being. Every child is a unique person of incredible complexity and intricate design, complete with immortal spirit, mind, and will, with vast potential and incalculable worth—wrought from that most intimate coming together of husband and wife. To call children a blessing, as the Bible consistently does, is an understatement.[59] The multiplication of children is one of God's chief purposes in marriage, yet merely having children is not enough; the Lord wants "godly offspring." To achieve this end, He designed marriage and the distinct roles of husband and wife to be the perfect environment for nurturing, training, and discipling godly offspring. Here's a little exercise to stir your vision. If you and your spouse raised six children to be godly offspring, and if each of them raised six godly offspring, and so on for five generations, the total number of devoted Christ-followers blessing and serving your nation would be 7,776! Think of the impact this could have on your nation and the world.

In our fallen world, children are seen not as a blessing but as a burden and a nuisance. They are seen as interfering with our rebellious and selfish desire for personal autonomy. Anti-children attitudes, in various degrees, are sadly found in the Church as well, with many married couples choosing to have fewer and fewer children. In many countries, particularly in Europe, Russia, and Japan, many couples have simply stopped having children altogether, and as a result, their cultures are literally dying.[60] Even cultures that are more traditionally associated with large families are falling below the replacement level of 2.1 children per family. Seventeen nations or territories in Latin America, as well as the United States, now fall below this level.[61]

Applying this principle in your life

Make a list of all the reasons you value children. Are you willing to make sacrifices in order to have children and to teach them the ways of the Lord? What are the most powerful challenges for you in dedicating yourself to raising children who love, honor, and obey the Lord? Is there an older Christian couple you know who have successfully raised children who are now living for Christ and serving the Lord? If not, ask your pastor for a recommendation of a couple with whom you could develop a friendship for support and counsel.

PRINCIPLE 3:
A fundamental duty of parents is to educate and disciple their children

The Bible stresses the importance of the family as *the primary training ground* for mature godly character. In the words of Philip Lancaster,

> Throughout the ages, the family has been the nursery of faith for each new generation, the primary place in which Christian discipleship has occurred. The future is shaped, generation-by-generation, in homes. The home is the primary arena for living out the Christian life. In the home, sin, hurt, reconciliation, and healing occur daily. In the home the ignorant are taught, the rebellious disciplined, the repentant restored, the hungry fed, the naked clothed, the sick healed. . . . The home is the place where proper roles and relationships are practiced.[62]

The Bible also teaches that parents bear the first and most fundamental responsibility for the education of their children. Certainly grandparents, church leaders, and schools can play important roles, but it is the father and mother who bear the *primary responsibility* and privilege. The most fundamental task of a mother and father is to show God to their children. Children know their parents before they know God. As parents open their hearts, love and train their children, walk with God openly before their families, and urge their children to follow the Lord with them, the children will have opportunities to experience God as a living reality in their own lives.[63]

God created the family to "be a community of teaching and learning about God and godliness."[64] To mothers and fathers, God says: "*You shall teach* [My ways, My commands and precepts] *diligently to your children, and shall talk of them when you sit in your house, and when you walk by the way, and when you lie down, and when you rise*" (Deuteronomy 6:6–8). This instruction must be more than head knowledge; it must be applied within the family, the church, and the community. The goal is for the commitment of the parents to God and His Word to pass from their hearts to the hearts of their children. This happens in the context of an intimate, discipleship relationship that continues at all times (from rising up to lying down) and in all places (at home and along the way).[65] Of course, the Bible must be the principal curriculum—its content, doctrine, and application to every area of life. Albert Mohler writes,

> The Bible presents a model of education that begins with the knowledge of God and then extends to a knowledge of God's law and the created order. All objects of knowledge and disciplines of study are made meaningful by the fact that God has created an intelligible universe that he intended his creatures to understand, at least in part.[66]

Both mothers and fathers share the responsibility to instruct their children. Proverbs 6:20–21 says: "*My son, keep your **father's** commandment, and forsake not our **mother's** teaching*" (emphasis added). It is critical that mother and father be united in this endeavor, yet the father, as household leader, has a critical role. "*And you, **fathers**, . . . bring them up in the training and admonition of the Lord*" (Ephesians 6:4, emphasis added). "The father's goal should be the hearts of his children. He wins their hearts by demonstrating sacrificial service, compassion, and tenderness; by washing his children's feet; and by setting aside his will in order to do what is best for them."[67] He is to shepherd his children, and to do this he must know the condition of his flock. It takes a great deal of time to discover what is in the heart of a child, but a father must make it his business to know. Only then can he give the kind of encouragement and instruction that will be most helpful. Discipline is also important as a form of corrective training, aimed at leading children beyond foolishness to self-controlled wisdom. Just as there is purposeful and loving discipline in God's family, the Church (Proverbs 3:11–12; Hebrews 12:5–11), so there must be in the human family.[68]

It should be the goal of every godly mother and father to prepare a quiver full of well-made "children arrows" (Psalm 127:4, 5), with which they can advance God's kingdom. Indeed, doing this is among the greatest privileges of parenting. As the parents devote themselves to molding and shaping their children to be disciples of Jesus, these children in turn influence their own children and grandchildren through many generations. *"His offspring will be mighty in the land; the generation of the upright will be blessed"* (Psalm 112:2).

Applying this principle in your life

Are you in agreement with God that He has made you, as parent, the primary teacher of your children? Ask Him to show you areas in which you have unconsciously yielded your authority and responsibility to the church, school, or government. Are you willing to embrace this role as your child's principal teacher of God and His ways? If so, the following chapters will help guide you in this role. Ask God to open your heart and mind to be renewed and to be released fully into this magnificent call upon your life together.

Closing Thoughts

Jonathan Edwards (1703–58) stands among the finest theologians, pastors, and intellectuals the United States has ever produced. He played a central role in the First Great Awakening, authored many books, preached countless sermons, and inspired generations of missionaries. Yet his greatest legacy is one he shares with his wife, Sarah—the amazing influence their godly offspring had on shaping the United States across many generations. Jonathan and Sarah Edwards are a prime example of how God can use the uniquely multi-generational institution of the family to bless an entire nation. In the span of 150 years, from this one couple came:

- Thirteen college presidents and sixty-five college professors

- One hundred lawyers and thirty judges

- Sixty-six medical doctors

- Three United States Senators, three state governors, three mayors of large cities, and a vice president of the United States.

- Leaders in banking, commerce, and industry

- Over one hundred cross-cultural missionaries.[69]

This kind of culture-shaping influence did not happen by accident. It is the fruit of a marriage built upon the teachings of the Bible. Could your family have a similar impact on your nation? A husband and wife who adopt this vision see in their children their most important mission in life.

> *"Children are a heritage from the Lord . . . like arrows in the hands of a warrior"* (Psalm 127:3, 4).

Arrows are weapons of war. Our children are likened to arrows in a battle against an enemy. The battle is for the advancement of God's kingdom and the discipling of nations. Our enemy is Satan. Why arrows? With a sword, a soldier can attack only as far as he can reach. But a properly made arrow can strike an enemy far beyond. Likewise, our children should far surpass us in their godly maturity and impact for Christ's kingdom. And their children should advance even further. Allow this to be your vision for your marriage and family—a vision to raise up a generation of warrior-servants who will advance boldly against the enemy in every sphere of society.

> *Heavenly Father, I understand more clearly than ever before that You hold me accountable to disciple my children for Christ, and that I have a generational duty to pass a godly legacy to my grandchildren and great grandchildren. My desire is to see my children leading godly lives and making noble contributions in society, but I need Your help and wisdom. I ask You this day to illumine my mind and equip me for the task at hand. Help me keep the*

long-term commitment and make the necessary changes in my life that will yield righteous fruit in my children, that we as a family can contribute to seeing the Earth filled with the knowledge of Your glory. Amen.

Additional Resources

Lancaster, Philip. *Family Man, Family Leader: Biblical Fatherhood as the Key to a Thriving Family,* San Antonio, Tex.: The Vision Forum, Inc., 2003.

Miller, Darrow L. *Nurturing the Nations: Reclaiming the Dignity and Divine Calling of Women in Building Healthy Cultures.* Downers Grove, Ill.: InterVarsity Press, 2012.

CHAPTER 5

THE POWER OF WORDS
AND GOD'S WORD

What is a word? We hear words, think words, speak words, sing words, and write words every day. But what is the essence of a word? How do words affect the development and health of our children, our families, and our nation? The answers to these questions may surprise you, as we consider what God has to say about the power of words and their enduring effect in our lives. The dictionary defines "word" as "a vocal sound or combination of sounds uttered by the human voice that, when combined with other words, express an idea."[70] In English, its root is a Greek word that means "to speak." However, words are more than units of language by which we communicate our thoughts. According to the Bible, words are invisible, powerful agents with the potential to produce life or death (Proverbs 18:21; Matthew 12:35–37). Words have incredible force. Words determine the course of our lives, our families, and our nations!

Words are the building blocks of ideas, and ideas have eternal consequences through the actions of individuals that shape their own destiny and the destiny of nations! Satan, the ruler of the world's system, uses words to war for the hearts and minds of people, particularly children. This war, which is fought not with guns and ammunition but with words and ideas, rages daily in our classrooms, in the media, and in the popular culture. It seeks to enslave our children on a daily basis. In most nations, the media is the primary disseminator of the ideas and values of a global, anti-Christian agenda. Social media, the internet, television, radio, magazines, and newspapers greatly influence the mindset and aesthetic tastes of both adults and children all over the world. Parents are losing this war from their lack of biblical knowledge and spiritual weapons; however, both parents and children can be equipped to combat ungodly influences and win the war of ideas. Victory requires recognizing the enemy's tactics and understanding the power of words. Words are the key to waging the battle and winning the victory.

power (n.) A force or energy; the faculty of moving or producing a change in something.

God spoke creation into existence by His Word

Creator God reveals Himself to man through His Word:

- His *spoken* word at creation

- His eternal, *living* Word, Jesus Christ

- His inspired *written* Word, the Bible

The book of Genesis begins with God speaking the universe into existence and naming each wondrous dimension of creation:

> *In the beginning* [before time began] *God created the heavens and the earth. And the earth was formless and void, and darkness was over the surface of the deep; and the Spirit of God was moving over the surface of the waters. Then* **God said,** *"Let there be light"; and there was light. God saw that the light was good; and God separated the light from the darkness. God called the light day, and the darkness He called night. And there was evening and there was morning, one day.* (Genesis 1:1–5)

God's words created the heavens and the Earth. What we see in the material world was made from that which is invisible: *"By faith, we understand that the worlds were prepared by the word of God, so that what is seen was not made out of things which are visible"* (Hebrews 11:3).

Jesus Christ, the Living Word, was present at creation

Jesus Christ is the Living Word who was present at creation. He created all things, and He holds all things together by the word of His power:

> *In the beginning* [before time began] *was the Word, and the Word was with God, and the Word was God. He was in the beginning with God. All things came into being by Him, and apart from Him nothing came into being that has come into being. In Him was life, and the life was the light of men. . . . And the Word became flesh, and dwelt among us, and we saw His glory, glory as of the only begotten from the Father, full of grace and truth.* (John 1:1–4, 14)

> *In these last days God has spoken to us in His Son, whom He appointed heir of all things, through whom also He made the world. And He is the radiance of His glory and the exact representation of His nature, and* **upholds all things by the word of His power.** (Hebrews 1:2, 3, emphasis added)

God created man in His image and endowed him with language

On the sixth day, God fashioned man in His own image as the crowning glory of creation (Genesis 1:26, 27; 2:7; Psalm 8:4–6). By His Holy Spirit, God breathed life into man (Genesis 2:7). He gave Adam the gift of language to communicate with Him and with others and to subdue the Earth. Man did not grunt like an animal, his inarticulate sounds gradually forming language, as Darwinism would have us believe.[71] At creation God endowed man with language, as well as with conscience, imagination, and the ability to reason. These attributes distinguish man from animals and ennoble man with immortal dignity.

God gave man words with which to build and govern a Word-centered (Christ-centered) family and culture

Initially, Adam was in perfect unity with God. Divine revelation governed his rational knowledge and informed his decisions and actions. God privileged Adam with accountability for naming the animals, by which Adam also established dominion over them. God fashioned a woman for Adam and placed them together in the garden of Eden to cultivate and enlarge it. God walked and communed with them, giving them supernatural knowledge. With words, God blessed them and commissioned them to rule the Earth. With words, He also warned them against disobeying His commands.

> God blessed them; and God said to them, "Be fruitful and multiply, and fill the earth, and subdue it; and rule over . . . every living thing that moves on the earth." (Genesis 1:28)

> Out of the ground the Lord God formed every beast of the field and every bird of the sky, and brought them to the man to see what he would call them; and whatever the man called a living creature, that was its name. (Genesis 2:19, 20)

Words are invisible, governing agents. They edify, instruct, and bless, or they tear down, deceive, and curse. God gave language as a tool for building and governing a righteous and just society, based upon His commands and principles. He commanded mankind to build a Word-centered life and culture through marriage and the family.

> For I have chosen him [Abraham], so that he may command his children and his household after him to keep the way of the Lord by doing righteousness and justice; so that the Lord may bring upon Abraham what He has spoken about him. (Genesis 18:19)

Sin broke Adam and Eve's relationship with God and launched a war of words

Adam and Eve were soon tested when the crafty serpent tempted Eve. He distorted God's words when he spoke to the woman, saying, "Indeed, has God said . . . ?" (Genesis 3:1–5). Eve entertained the serpent's twisted words and became deceived. Adam disobeyed God and ate the fruit. The unity they had enjoyed with God was broken. Their now-corrupted reasoning was ruled by their own rational knowledge. Sin polluted their imaginations and their perception of God, themselves, and the world.

> They heard the sound of the Lord God walking in the garden in the cool of the day, and the man and his wife hid themselves from

*the presence of the Lord God among the trees of the garden. Then
the Lord God called to the man, and said to him, "Where are you?"
And Adam said, "I heard the sound of You in the garden, and I
was afraid because I was naked; so I hid myself."* (Genesis 3:8–10)

Sin corrupts our thinking and our choices. It leaves us self-centered,
not God-centered! Sin destroys relationships. In the garden, Satan's
lies distorted God's truth in the hearts of Adam and Eve, and their
spoken words revealed the effect of their deception. They exchanged
the truth of the kingdom of God for the lies of the world's kingdom. Jesus said, *"The mouth speaks out of that which fills the heart"*
(Matthew 12:34). Deception, fear, and guilt filled their hearts and influenced their thoughts, words, and actions. Adam and Eve became
afraid of God and tried to hide from Him who is Truth. A cosmic
struggle was initiated between truth and error, light and darkness,
the kingdom of God and the kingdom of this world (Romans 3:9–18,
23). A war of words and ideas[72] was launched on the battlefield of the
mind of man. That war continues to this day.

God mercifully removed Adam and Eve from the garden, lest they
should eat of the tree of life and be alienated from God forever. Theologians call this disobedience the "Fall of man." Adam and Eve introduced brokenness into the human race (Romans 5:12–21). Therefore,
we are all born in this fallen state. Our ability to reason is corrupted
(Jeremiah 17:9); we are *"dead in our transgressions and sins"* (Ephesians 2:1). Our spirits must be *"born again"* by the Spirit of God
(John 3:1–21). God cursed the serpent and the soil. He sentenced the
woman to suffer in childbirth and the man to toil by the sweat of his
brow. He also promised salvation and redemption through the seed
of the woman (Genesis 3:14–19)—His only begotten Son, *"the living
and eternal Word."* In God's fullness of time, Christ clothed Himself
with flesh to purchase salvation for sinful man with His blood.

Words are the building blocks of ideas

God designed us to think and to express our thoughts with words.
Words direct our thinking and reasoning. They inspire ideas. These
ideas influence our choices and actions every day! Words and ideas
set the course of our lives. When we define words biblically, we think
and reason with God's truth, which frees us from the bondage of the

world's system. When we define them according to the world's system, they lead to deception, bondage, and impoverishment.

Ideas have consequences for good or evil

Thoughts always try to express themselves in actions. *"As a man thinks within himself, so he is"* (Proverbs 23:7). Our life story and our character emanate from our choices, which are based on our view of God, life, and priorities. In other words, our worldview determines the choices we make, and those choices build our character and our life. Ideas based on the lies of this fallen world impoverish individuals, families, and nations. They lead to bondage, conflict, and spiritual death. Ideas based on God's principles bless individuals, families, and nations with truth that produces liberty, peace, and spiritual life.

The Old Testament includes a compelling example of how words build ideas that produce serious, multigenerational consequences. The book of Numbers relates the story of twelve leaders whom Moses sent to spy out the Promised Land. God had miraculously delivered the Israelites from 400 years of slavery in Egypt (the world's system) and pointed them toward the Promised Land. Moses wanted to know what they would encounter there: Were the inhabitants strong or weak? Few or many? Was the land fortified? Fruitful or barren? For forty days, the men surveyed the territory and returned with a report and samples of luscious fruit.

Ten spies issued an "evil" report (Numbers 14:37). They said, *"Indeed, the land flows with milk and honey, but the cities are large and well fortified, and the people are strong and of great size, making us seem as small as grasshoppers."* The Israelites responded in fear and disbelief. The other two spies, Caleb and Joshua, tried to calm the people with words of faith, saying, *"The land which we passed through to spy out is an exceedingly good land. . . . We should by all means go up and take possession of it, for we will surely overcome it"* (Numbers 14:7, 8; 13:30).

The people rebelled and cried out, *"If only we had died in Egypt or in this desert!"* (Numbers 14:2, NIV). God responded, *"As I live, just as you have spoken in My hearing, so I will surely do to you"* (Numbers 14:28). God had performed mighty miracles in Egypt, parted the Red Sea, and delivered them from slavery. Angered at their unbelief, He issued an indictment: they would never enter the Promised Land.

The ten spies who spoke the evil report soon died from a plague. With the exceptions of only Caleb and Joshua, who were preserved by God to enter the Promised Land and receive His promised inheritance (Joshua 3; 14:14), the entire multitude of Israelites over the age of twenty died in the wilderness. An eleven-day journey took forty years! All twelve leaders surveyed the same Promised Land. All agreed on the facts. But only Joshua and Caleb believed God's word and by faith delivered a good report based on God's promises. This account teaches us that words are the substance of ideas. Ideas, indeed, have consequences for good or evil.

PRINCIPLE 1:
Language is first learned through imitation

Each child is God's gift to a set of parents (Psalm 127:3), who are the child's first and most influential teachers. The infant first learns language by imitating the words spoken by his parents. As he mimics the sounds, his parents teach him their meaning. His vocabulary grows, and the family's heritage and values are passed along to the next generation. The young child's view of the world around him begins to form. When parents teach God's Word and principles, they influence the child's vocabulary and ideas and nurture him with a godly heritage and a biblical worldview. If God's Word and principles are not taught, the young one develops the worldview of the ungodly system around him.

Beginning with Abraham, God commanded fathers to teach their *"children and their household . . . to keep the way of the Lord by doing righteousness and justice"* (Genesis 18:19; Ephesians 6:4). God holds parents accountable for their children's education. Parents are to teach His Word to their children and their grandchildren (Deuteronomy 4:9), so they in turn will become godly members of society and disciple their own families and nation for Christ.

> *"These words, which I am commanding you today, shall be on your heart; and you shall teach them diligently to your sons and shall talk of them when you sit in your house and when you walk by the way and when you lie down and when you rise up."* (Deuteronomy 6:6, 7)

Our words and their accompanying actions affect a child's tender soul. Some words convey love, affirmation, and joy, while others issue warnings and instructions. Some words are sung softly to music, others spoken with great force. Destructive words conveyed in anger lodge in the child's heart and are "heard" again and again throughout his life. As God's people, we can apply this principle by imitating Christ and using His words to nurture a loving, righteous family. God calls us to be *culture builders* by first knowing Him and His Word and then by revealing Christ through our words and actions, both at home and in public life. As we imitate Christ and apply His words, our children will imitate us.

Applying this principle in your life

The following suggestions have great potential to affect your young children's thoughts, sensibilities, habits, actions, and character development. If practiced, your leadership in these areas will prepare them for a place of Christian leadership and service among their peers.

1. Read the Scriptures aloud to your baby in the womb. God's Word nourishes the unborn child's spirit and plants a love for God's Word in your baby.

2. Pray God's Word for your children daily.

3. Agree with what Christ says about children and speak His life-giving words aloud to your children on a regular basis. Bless them aloud! Affirm and call forth their full potential in Christ often!

4. Read and sing God's Word, children's lullabies, poems, and stories with Christian ideals to your young ones on a daily basis.

5. Complete key word studies during your devotions. Dig into the meanings of words as God uses them in Scripture. Use this vocabulary when speaking to your children.

6. Hold family worship and Bible study fellowship on a regular basis in your home. Teach the meanings of biblical words and passages to your children.

7.   Memorize God's promises together with your little ones.

8.   As your children learn to read, direct them to read God's Word daily and meditate on its truth. Building these habits into your children at an early age nurtures a lifelong love of God and His Word.

PRINCIPLE 2:
Life and death are in the power of the tongue

The tongue has tremendous power to create or destroy. The Bible, especially the books of Proverbs and James, provides much wisdom about the use of our tongue. When we act in the flesh, we carelessly speak destructive words. Words burrow deeply into the hearts of the hearer (Proverbs 23:16). Hurtful words distort our identity as a child of God and thwart our full potential. Kind, thoughtful words are just as powerful. They encourage, edify, and restore broken relationships.

> *Death and life are in the power of the tongue, and those who love it will eat its fruit.* (Proverbs 18:21)

> *My inmost being will rejoice, when your lips speak what is right.* (Proverbs 23:16)

> *It is the Spirit who gives life; the flesh profits nothing; the words that I have spoken to you are spirit and are life.* (John 6:63)

The tongue is difficult to tame. James teaches that *"the tongue is a small part of the body which defiles the entire body, and sets on fire the course of our life. No one can tame the tongue; it is a restless evil and full of deadly poison. With it we bless our Lord and Father, and with it we curse men, who have been made in the likeness of God"* (James 3:1–11). He compares the tongue to a ship's rudder; though small, it steers a large vessel.

Word problems are heart problems!

What proceeds from our tongue is an indication of the condition of our heart. Jesus taught us:

> *"The good man out of the good treasure of his heart brings forth what is good; and the evil man out of the evil treasure brings*

forth what is evil; for his mouth speaks from that which fills his heart." (Luke 6:45)

"But I tell you, that every careless word that people speak, they shall give an accounting for it in the day of judgment. For by your words you will be justified, and by your words you will be condemned." (Matthew 12:36, 37)

"Word problems are heart problems. Within each of our hearts there is a war between two kingdoms—the kingdom of self and the kingdom of God. One of the two is always ruling our heart and shaping our speech. Only when our heart is ruled by love will our tongue overflow with wholesome and loving words."[73] Loving speech requires a lifetime of meditation in God's Word and yielding to His Spirit day by day. Unless God's Spirit abides in our heart, no lasting change is possible because our flesh rules over our heart and shapes our talk. Fallen man cannot change his stony, sinful heart. He must receive a new heart. He must be *"born again,"* as Jesus instructed Nicodemus (John 3:1–21).

God instructs us to *"watch over"* our heart, *"for from it flow the springs of life"* (Proverbs 4:23). In other words, guard what you read, what you watch on television, what you listen to, what you meditate on during your quiet moments. Guard your attitudes. Watch for selfishness, anger, bitterness, unforgiveness, and criticism. These seeds produce abusive, unwholesome speech and lead to unstable, dysfunctional relationships. As parents, we are also accountable to God to guard what our children read, watch, speak, and do.

Bless your children every day

God intended words to create, to save, and to bless by faith. The act of blessing originates in God's heart toward us, His children. It involves the spoken word, which conveys prosperity and spiritual heritage. Throughout the book of Genesis, God invoked blessings: He blessed man at creation (Genesis 1:28); He blessed Noah and his sons (Genesis 9:1); Abraham, in whom all the families of the Earth were blessed (Genesis 12); his wife, Sarah, the mother of nations; Isaac (Genesis 26); Jacob (Genesis 28; 32); and Joseph (Genesis 39). This was a blessed family, the progenitors of God's chosen people! In the Gospels, Jesus blessed untold numbers of people. His Sermon on the Mount[74] paints the picture of kingdom life through a series of blessings. His tender ministry toward children always included a blessing, as He laid His hands on their heads and spoke His life-giving words into their spirit.

> And they were bringing children to Him so that He might touch them; and the disciples rebuked them. But when Jesus saw this, He was indignant and said to them, "Permit the children to come to Me; do not hinder them; for the kingdom of God belongs to such as these.". . . And He took them in His arms and began blessing them, laying His hands upon them. (Mark 10:13–16)

Jesus redeemed us from the curse of the Law in order that in Him the blessing of Abraham might come to the Gentiles, so that we could receive the promise of the Spirit through faith (Galatians 3:13, 14).

To be blessed by one's parents is to have an inner security and confidence throughout life. To be unblessed is to live restlessly and inadequately, with an inner poverty! Many of God's children endure a lifetime without blessing, perpetually seeking peace and happiness. In the Old Testament, Jacob, Isaac's son, is the prototype of the unblessed child. He stole his older brother's blessing without receiving the sense of wellbeing he anticipated. He lived restlessly for the greater part of his life, until God instructed him to return to his own country. Concerned that his brother might be seeking revenge, he stopped to pray. A "man" appeared and wrestled with him until daybreak. Jacob would not let him go until the man blessed him. This "man" was the pre-incarnate Jesus Christ, who did, indeed, bless Jacob and changed his name to "Israel." When he cried out, "*I will not let you go until you bless me!*" he was finally blessed and received wholeness. Jacob reconciled with his brother (Genesis 33), blessed the pharaoh of Egypt (Genesis 47:5), and blessed his own son Joseph (Genesis 49:22–27). At the end of his life, Jacob blessed his grandchildren (Genesis 49:9–11, 16).

Blessing is a supernatural act that makes the impossible possible! Each generation must bless and empower the next. Every father must bless each of his children by laying his hands on the child's head and speaking aloud the life-giving gift of inner strength and happiness. In many cultures, a blessing is imparted as youth enter adulthood. While it is never too late to begin blessing your children, parents should bless their children at birth and continue to bless them routinely throughout their youth.

> *To sum up, all of you be harmonious, sympathetic, brotherly, kind-hearted, and humble in spirit; not returning evil for evil or insult for insult, but giving a blessing instead; for you were called for the very purpose that you might inherit a blessing.* (1 Peter 3:8, 9)

Applying this principle in your life

1. Complete a study of the tongue from the book of Proverbs. Create two columns, labeling one "The Foolish Tongue" and the other "The Wise Tongue." For children, use the AMO® Proverbs teacher guide to instruct them in the use of their tongue and the power of words. The guide also has Parent Prayer and Blessing cards you can use with your children. (It is available in English, Spanish, and Portuguese.)

2. Forgive those who have hurt you with their words. Ask God to heal you, and receive His healing by faith.

3. Reflect on the condition of your own heart. Ask the Holy Spirit to reveal to you anyone you have offended with your words. Go to them and ask their forgiveness.

4. Begin to bless your children individually. Write out blessings for each one, using God's richest promises in the Bible. Call each one to yourself, lay your hands on his or her head, and speak aloud your life-giving words. Watch as God meets you in this act of empowerment to birth new life and joy in these most precious relationships.

PRINCIPLE 3:
Using God's Word effectively builds a Christ-centered life and family

As we wage the battle for the hearts and minds of our children with God's Word, He can rebuild broken relationships and restore unstable families. God's Word is alive and has spiritual energy. God's truth has power to renew our minds and tame our tongues.

For the word of God is living and active and sharper than any two-edged sword, and piercing as far as the division of soul and spirit, of both joints and marrow, and able to judge the thoughts and intentions of the heart. (Hebrews 4:12)

Incline your ear and hear the words of the wise and apply your mind to my knowledge; for it will be pleasant if you keep them within you, that they may be ready on your lips. (Proverbs 22:17, 18)

"If you abide in Me and My words abide in you, ask whatever you wish, and it will be done for you." (John 15:7)

How can the power of God's truth be released in our minds and hearts if we don't know His Word? We need to read the Bible every day to feed our spirit, renew our thinking, and receive God's guidance for our lives and family.

We are also instructed to meditate on His Word daily and submit to its wisdom to guide our personal decisions. The Hebrew word for "meditate" means "ponder, muse, rehearse in one's mind, study, converse with oneself aloud, and speak."[75] To meditate on God's Word is to agree with its truth and speak it aloud. God instructed Joshua, one of the two faithful spies, to meditate on His Word day and night so he could be a wise and successful leader and prosper among the pagans of Canaan. "Prosper" in the Hebrew does not necessarily refer to material wealth but means "to accomplish what is intended by God." Joshua's decisions were informed by meditating on God's Word. After the Israelites conquered Canaan, Joshua wrote, *"Not one of the good promises which the Lord had made to the house of Israel failed; all came to pass"* (Joshua 21:45). Joshua's faithfulness to meditate on God's Word was the key to his success as Israel's leader.

"This book of the law shall not depart from your mouth, but you shall meditate on it day and night, so that you may be careful to do according to all that is written in it; for then you will make your way prosperous, and then you will have success." (Joshua 1:8)

The battle for the hearts and minds of our children is not fleshly but spiritual. Therefore, our weapons must be spiritual. Parents must learn how to use these invisible and supernatural weapons that God has provided to guard and protect their children. The primary weapon is God's Word. Parents need to become "Word warriors" and actively fight for the spiritual health of their family and particularly of their children. This is the first line of defense that God provides for securing the wellbeing of our children.

> For though we walk in the flesh, we do not war according to the flesh, for the weapons of our warfare are not of the flesh, but divinely powerful for the destruction of fortresses. We are destroying speculations and every lofty thing raised up against the knowledge of God, and we are taking every thought captive to the obedience of Christ. (2 Corinthians 10:3–5)

> Put on the full armor of God, that you will be able to stand firm against the schemes of the devil. For our struggle is not against flesh and blood, but against the rulers, against the powers, against the world forces of this darkness, against the spiritual forces of wickedness in the heavenly places. (Ephesians 6:11, 12)

Paul describes these spiritual weapons (Ephesians 6:13–18), including "the shield of faith and the sword of the Spirit, which is the word of God" (v. 17). The sword of the Spirit is both defensive and offensive, defeating the enemy's tactics and releasing the power and purposes God has for His Word.

> "So is my word that goes out from my mouth: It will not return to me empty, but will accomplish what I desire and achieve the purpose for which I sent it." (Isaiah 55:11 NIV)

God's truth is the key to transformation! God's Word is eternal seed, able to reproduce itself when properly planted and cultivated in the soil of our hearts. Read Jesus' Parable of the Sower in Mark 4:1–20. A farmer who wants to harvest corn plants corn seed, not apple seed. He clears his land of rocks and carefully tills the soil before planting his precious seed. He fertilizes and waters the seed and guards the young, tender plants from insects and weeds as they mature. He harvests the fruit and prudently saves seed for next year's crop. So it is with parents. If we desire righteous children with a Christian mindset, imagination, and character, we must lead our children to Christ, till the soil of their minds, and plant God's Word in their hearts. As these tender plants begin to grow, we must continuously fertilize, water, and guard them throughout their formative years.

You have been born again not of seed which is perishable, but imperishable, that is, through the living and enduring word of God. (1 Peter 1:23)

How blessed is the man who does not walk in the counsel of the wicked, nor stand in the path of sinners, nor sit in the seat of scoffers! But his delight is in the law of the Lord, and in His law he meditates day and night. He will be like a tree firmly planted by streams of water, which yields its fruit in its season and its leaf does not wither; and in whatever he does, he prospers. The wicked are not so, but they are like chaff which the wind drives away. (Psalm 1:1–4)

Applying this principle in your life

Life-producing words have the power to rebuild broken lives, families, and cultures.

1. Measure the time you devote to cultural influences: television, magazines, movies, radio, computer games, music, telephone, books, sports, etc. Compare this to the time you spend in God's Word and the time you actively engage with your spouse and children.

2. Assess the spiritual state of each of your children. Write a realistic plan to wage the battle for their hearts and minds, referencing the above principles.

3. Develop a personal prayer journal, listing each family member by name. Claim God's promises for each one and pray the Word daily. Record the answers to your prayers.

Closing Thoughts

What is God saying about the spiritual condition of your family? What has He shown you about the words of your mouth and the meditation of your heart? We have all failed as parents and fallen short of God's standard for our speech. But we are not without help. Change begins with God's forgiveness. *"If we confess our sins, He is faithful and righteous to forgive us our sins and to cleanse us from all unrighteousness"* (1 John 1:9). Lift your burdens to the Lord and pray right now. If needed, use the following simple prayer:

> *Dear Lord Jesus, I invite You into my heart anew right now. Please be gracious to me according to Your lovingkindness. Please forgive my failure to build a Christ-centered family. Like Isaiah, I am a man of unclean lips, living among a people of unclean lips. I have often hurt You and others, especially my spouse and my children, with careless and destructive words. I turn from my sinful ways and habits. Thank You for your grace and help in time of need. Cleanse my tongue and place in my heart a hunger for Your Word. Help me guard the words of my mouth and become a "Word warrior" in my home. May the words of my mouth and the meditation of my heart find acceptance in Your sight, my Rock and my Redeemer. Amen.*

Additional Resources

Meyer, Joyce. *The Secret Power of Speaking God's Word.* New York: Faith Words, 2004.

Piper, John, Justin Taylor, Paul Tripp, and Sinclair B. Ferguson. *The Power of Words and the Wonder of God.* Wheaton, Ill.: Crossway Books, 2009.

Sherrill, John. *He Still Speaks Today: Releasing the Dynamic Power of God's Word in Your Life.* Seattle, Wash.: YWAM Publishing, 1997.

Taulbert, Clifton L. *Eight Habits of the Heart: Embracing the Values that Build Strong Families and Communities.* New York: The Penguin Group, 1996.

CHAPTER 6

THE CHRISTIAN VIEW
OF CHILDREN

Jesus has a remarkable view of children. He told His disciples that whoever humbles himself like a child is the "greatest in the kingdom of God."[76] Jesus modeled the Father's view of children in the oft-told incident reported in Mark 10:13–16:

And they were bringing children to Him so that He might touch them; but the disciples rebuked them. But when Jesus saw this, He was indignant and said to them, "Permit the children to come to Me; do not hinder them; for the kingdom of God belongs to such as these. Truly I say to you, whoever does not receive the kingdom of God like a child will not enter it at all." And He took them in His arms and began blessing them, laying His hands on them.

child (n.) The progeny of parents; one created in the image of God who is young in grace; unfixed in principles; and weak in knowledge, judgment, and experience.

Jesus loves children and interacted with them by lovingly holding them, blessing them, and healing them. He modeled how parents are to behave toward their own children.

The cultures of the world do not value children as God does

In every nation of the world, Christian parents' views of children have been powerfully influenced by their culture and personal experiences. Our thinking about children has been unconsciously shaped by what we see, hear, and absorb from the values of the culture around us. Often these beliefs run counter to biblical truth, yet they are grievously present in the Church and even advocated by the Church.

The shameful tragedy of our time is that in too many instances children are despised. Never before in the history of mankind have more babies been aborted, abandoned, abused, violated, exploited, malnourished, diseased, traded, and forced into armed combat. Children of the twenty-first century are too often considered a curse rather than a reward, a burden rather than a blessing. They are used as political pawns and property to be traded or discarded. The United Nations and other global organizations advocate birth control, sterilization, and abortion as "solutions" to the problems of birth defects, diseases, and insufficient food and water. The biblical principle is quite the opposite: *Societies that hold children in low esteem reap economic and cultural impoverishment.* This is pictured in the fact that the number of births in many countries has dropped below the 2.1 replacement fertility rate.[77] Entire nations are dying.

The neglect and abuse of today's child have devastated not only his physical being but also his very soul. Given the brokenness of the family and the materialistic priorities of parents, little but "crumbs" are left for the child's heart. Globally, one-quarter to one-third of all families are headed by single mothers with very little time and energy to nurture their children. Even when fathers are present, studies indicate that the typical father spends less than five minutes a day with his children. While God's covenant plan is to pass along His blessings through earthly fathers, the current generation is pitifully known as the "fatherless generation."

Increasing numbers of couples choose to delay having children and to have very few children, so that both parents can generate income. Indeed, it is hard to live on less. It takes character and commitment. Pastors need to make Christian family life and God's view of children a priority in their teaching and preaching. If we value and nurture the priceless gift of children, our families and nation will prosper in every sphere of life.

God's view of children is rooted in creation and covenant

The Bible presents a view of children radically different from that of today's global culture. Created in the image of God, each one is ennobled with dignity and worth.[78] God's mandate to the first man and woman on Earth was, *"Be fruitful and multiply; fill the earth and govern it"* (Genesis 1:28). Children are the fruit most highly esteemed by the Lord. *"Children are a gift of the Lord, the fruit of the womb is a reward"* (Psalm 127:3). They are given to families as a great blessing: *"All these blessings will come upon you and overtake you if you obey the Lord your God: Blessed shall be the offspring of your body"* (Deuteronomy 28:2, 4a).

The first mention of the word "child" in Scripture is in reference to Abraham's wife, Sarah, being barren.[79] Despite his and her advanced ages, Abraham believed God's promise of a son who would be his heir. In fact, God promised Abraham many descendants, as many as the stars in the heavens.[80] As Abraham looked up into the night sky full of lights too many to count, he must have gazed in wonder and worshipful awe. The longing of his heart had been for a child, and God had spoken to him of so much more. God said, *"I will make you very fruitful; I will make nations of you, and kings will come from you"* (Genesis 17:6). Abraham waited in faith for twenty-five years before the covenant promise of a son was fulfilled in the joyful birth of Isaac.

Children are to be desired and gratefully received as a trust so precious that it has no adequate standard of measure. Parents, along with the Church, are to invest in these young ones with all our spiritual life and earthly resources as the number one priority in family, church, and society. Each child deserves to be cherished as a promise of God's unfolding plan of redemption. Every child has a vital place in His story.

The instruction and discipleship of children in the Christian faith is the heart of the Christian father's covenant with God

The instruction and discipleship of children is the very means by which God has chosen to advance His covenant plan. It is noteworthy that God linked the meaning of Abram's name, "father," to His covenant in Genesis 17:4: *"As for Me, behold, My **covenant** is with you, and you will be the **father** of a multitude of nations"* (emphasis added). In fact, in the subsequent verse God changed Abram's name to Abraham, which means *"father of a multitude."* God's covenant is centered in and dependent on *fatherhood.* Families are in crisis today because of the loss of revelation about covenant and the deterioration in commitment to fulfill the role of father. When fathers do not provide godly leadership in the family, the knowledge of God fails to be transmitted to the next generation. What is God's solution to this crisis? The answer begins with the restoration of "the hearts of the fathers to their children" (Malachi 4:6). Single mothers, be sure to read the special note to you in Appendix I.

In Genesis 18:19, God says of Abraham, *"For I have chosen him, so that he may command his children and his household after him to keep the way of the Lord by doing righteousness and justice, so that the Lord may bring upon Abraham what He has spoken about him."*

> Will we see the king in our children? Will we invest our lives in the leaders of this upcoming generation?
> —BETTA MENGISTU

God rewarded Abraham's faith and obedience in teaching his children the ways of God by giving him countless descendants who became leaders of nations. King David came from Abraham's line, as did Jesus Christ. God's covenant with fathers today is the same as it was with Abraham: to make Christian fathers fruitful and to bring nations and kings from them. God's mandate to fill and govern the Earth is obeyed when parents see divine purpose in their children and disciple them in His ways. God's glory will be revealed through Christian families who cover the Earth. As families go, so goes the nation.

Children are created by God to learn best from their parents

A biblical definition for "child" is "one created in the image of God[81] who is young in grace;[82] unfixed in principles;[83] and weak in knowledge, judgment, and experience."[84] The human infant is more dependent on his parents for survival and growth than is the infant of any other creature. The human infant's brain is less developed at birth than that of any of the animals. God created the child full of potential to learn from his parents and fulfill God's special purposes. God designed the child to receive instruction from his parents for life, relationships, and eternity.

Young children have a God-given desire for human relationship, the cradle of learning. Within the special bonds of relationship with parents, the child learns that he is loved and cherished. He grows with a sure sense of security. Within the embrace of parental love and delight, the young child imitates his parents' language, social patterns, values, character, and worship. Each child is fearfully and wonderfully made in his mother's womb.[85]

Did you know that the unborn child is learning even before birth? While being formed in that secret place, he grows to recognize his parents' voices and respond to their words. He is nourished as the Word of God is read aloud and beautiful music is played in his home. He hears his parents praying for him and feels their touch through the mother's belly. At birth the babe will naturally attend to his mother's face and turn to his parents' voices.

> **parent** (n.) A father or mother; he or she that produces young. The duties of parents to their children are to maintain, protect, and educate them. When parents are wanting in authority, children are wanting in duty.

The tenderness of the bond that unites parents to their children is evidenced in the many Hebrew words for "child," of which there are at least twenty![86] *Children who begin life with this foundation of love, trust, and security learn more quickly and develop socially, intellectually, and spiritually.* The mother and father's love for God is naturally communicated to and experienced by the child in all they do together. This in turn opens the child's spirit to want to understand what his parents are saying and to imitate what they are doing. How wondrous are the ways God has designed children to learn from their parents!

Each child is fashioned by God for an appointed time and place in His story

God has a plan and a purpose for the life of each child. *"He chose us in Him before the foundation of the world"* (Ephesians 1:4). Young king Josiah's call was prophesied three centuries before his birth.[87] Before Jeremiah was formed in the womb, God appointed him a prophet to the nations.[88] Paul of the New Testament was "set apart even from his mother's womb" (Galatians 1:15). Samson, John the Baptist, and Jesus are other biblical examples of God's divine purpose being revealed prior to birth. These children are not exceptions. God chooses the time in history each child will be born, his parents, and the geographic setting of each child's birth. These factors are intentionally selected to accomplish a particular purpose within His glorious plan. Esther's uncle Mordecai challenged her to be ready to yield her life for the salvation of her people: *"Who knows whether you have not come to the kingdom for such a time as this?"* (Esther 4:14b ESV). The fulfillment of divine purpose results from knowing God and walking in His ways.

God's purpose for children of the twenty-first century requires parents who are committed to nurturing children with a passionate heart for the living God. During the time of Jeremiah in 640 B.C., an eight-year-old boy named Josiah was crowned king of Judah.[89] Both Josiah's father and grandfather were wicked kings, but his great-grandfather was a righteous king and religious reformer. Josiah's mother, Jedidah, must have been a godly woman who had a profound influence on her son. Josiah reigned as king in Jerusalem for 31 years, and *"he did right in the sight of the Lord"* (2 Kings 22:2). As a youth he began to pray earnestly for his nation. God put it in his heart to restore the house of the Lord. The Word of God was thus discovered buried in the temple. When Josiah heard the Word of God read, he was struck with grief that his nation had failed to obey God's commandments and had fallen into such moral decay. The Word of God provoked a revolution in Josiah's way of thinking and in his priorities as king. Josiah restored God's Word back to his people and led the greatest spiritual and cultural reformation in Israel's history before the coming of Jesus Christ.

God is looking for parents who are inspired to rear children like Josiah, children whose hearts are zealous for the Lord's righteousness and justice. He desires an entire generation of Josiahs to be taught to think and reason with truth from the Word. God is calling a generation of young men and women who will embrace His kingdom vision and principles and respond with passion, wisdom, obedience, and love for God. They are destined to become godly citizens of their nations and leaders in every sphere of society, reforming their cultures for Christ.

PRINCIPLE 1:
Every child needs unconditional love and salvation from his sinful nature, which God has provided through His Son

The Bible teaches that all children have inherited a sinful nature through the sin of Adam and Eve.[90] Therefore, every child needs to receive God's love and salvation by faith in the sacrifice of Jesus Christ for his sins.[91] The covenant that God makes with a father when He accepts Christ is not only for himself, but also for his household. The Lord commanded Noah, *"Enter the ark, you and all your household"* (Genesis 7:1). *"By faith Noah . . . prepared an ark for the saving of his house"* (Hebrews 11:7). In God's sight, the family is regarded as a unity under the headship of the father. *"I will establish My covenant between Me and you and your descendants after you throughout their generations for an everlasting covenant, to be God to you and to your descendants after you"* (Genesis 17:7).

It is the obedient faith of the father that releases God's grace to the whole family. It was Noah's faith that opened the way of salvation for his family. His faith was evidenced by his obedience in taking his family into the ark with him. It was Abraham's faith in God's promises for himself and his children, and his obedience in teaching God's ways to his children that enabled God to fulfill that which he had spoken. God's covenant is with the man and his descendants. The children of Christian parents are *"like Isaac* [Abraham's son], *children of promise"* (Galatians 4:28). Christian parents have confidence based on the Word that they will lead their child to know God for himself.

Applying this principle in your life

1. If you have not received Jesus Christ as your Lord and Savior, consider that God is calling you and your whole family with you. *"Believe on the Lord Jesus, and you will be saved, you and your household"* (Acts 16:31).

2. Read and obey God's Word so that your life will demonstrate to your child the blessings, love, and wisdom of God. The power of parental training lies in who we are and in our way of living before our children.

3. Seek God's wisdom for how to lead your child to want to know God.

4. Pray for your child's salvation from the moment of his conception.

PRINCIPLE 2:
**Every child needs a vision for what he can become,
and someone to cultivate his individuality, call it forth,
and believe God with him for its fulfillment**

Each child is unique, with a divine calling. Each child needs to know that he has been fashioned by God for an appointed time and place in His story. Sometimes God takes the initiative to speak His purpose to the parents, as He did with the parents of Samson, John the Baptist, and Jesus. When Samson's parents were told they would have a child, the father implored, *"Teach us what to do for the boy who is to be born"* (Judges 13:8b).

Certain preparation is alike for all children, but each child is uniquely fashioned for a particular purpose and place in God's story. Therefore, parents need to ask God for guidance and wisdom. Parents are called to recognize and affirm each child's individuality and call forth the gifts and attributes of that particular child. Each child is a tender planting of the Lord, needing cultivation. The heart of the child is to be guarded by parents from destructive forces. His spirit and soul are to be fed with truth and virtuous learning experiences that will develop his potential in Christ.

Applying this principle in your life

1. Teach your child about the children and youth in the Bible, how each one was an individual with his own unique abilities given by God for His purpose and plan.

2. Teach your child Scriptures related to the formation of God's personal plan for him before the foundation of the world. Instill in him wonder and a desire to know and fulfill God's plan for his life.

3. Seek God in prayer, asking that your child may discover and embrace his purpose and for Scriptures to pray during his childhood and youth.

4. While your child is young, engage him in activities that affirm his individuality. For example, dip his fingers in tempera paint and make fingerprints—there are no other

fingerprints in the world quite like his, nor is there an identical face, voice, or handwriting. Plan creative activities that will reflect his unique expression. He is one of a kind!

5. Cultivate the gifts and interests of your child. Write down one of his stories before he can write it himself. After studying Proverbs, have him write his own! Identify the God-given talents and natural abilities in your child and call them forth, both with words of encouragement and with learning experiences.

PRINCIPLE 3:
God builds from the inside out. The heart is the child's command center and governs his will and choices

A child's life flows from his heart, from the inside out. As parents, we need to cultivate truth, love, goodness, and beauty in the child's heart, and guard him from influences that would rob his heart of life. *"Watch over your heart with all diligence, for from it flow the springs of life"* (Proverbs 4:23). The aim of parents should be to help the child learn to govern his own heart according to the principles of life in the kingdom of God. God's kingdom is based on His righteousness and justice and is motivated by love. A reverence for the authority of Christ must be established in the parent's heart in order for it to be imparted to the child's heart. God wants children to learn obedience out of a heart of love for Him and for their parents. Habits precede the understanding of principles. A child whose habits are self-governing will be receptive to instruction in the principles of God's Word. A child can be taught how to exercise his will in governing his thinking, choices, decisions, conduct, and property.

Applying this principle in your life

1. Let your child know that he has been given to you by God in covenant. Be gentle but firm in communicating that this is the reason you cannot give way to his will when it is sinful. You have promised God to bring him up in a way that will please the Lord.

2. Explain to your child that choosing obedience to God's
    Law is a choice for life, peace, and blessing. Inspire your
    child toward obedience, toward valuing what God values,
    so that he increasingly wills in his own heart what God
    wills.

3. Nurture your child's heart with classic children's litera-
    ture whose characters demonstrate the joy of life when
    they chose God's ways. Talk with your child about how
    his ideas determine his choices, and how those choices
    have consequences.

4. When discipline is necessary, give it in love, not when
    you are upset. Show patient and consistent confidence
    in your child's ability to make wise choices.

PRINCIPLE 4:
Children need biblical truths and vocabulary
as the foundation upon which to worship God
and to imagine and reason Christianly

Fashioned in God's image, man was gifted at creation with language.
(See chapter five.) God gave man language primarily as a way to fellowship with Him and to praise and worship Him. We use language
to reason, communicate, govern, and bless others. As a child learns
the biblical definitions of words, his mind becomes conformed to the
truth and protected from the deception and impoverishment of the
culture around him. The foundation of the child's ability to imagine,
think, and reason Christianly is rooted in his familiarity with biblical words and Christian ideals. *"And do not be conformed to this
world, but be transformed by the renewing of your mind, so that you
may prove what the will of God is, that which is good and acceptable
and perfect"* (Romans 12:2). Transformation occurs from the inside
out. As the child's thoughts are filled with God's thoughts and God's
words, his own ideas are formed and his choices and behavior begin
to reflect those ideas.

Cultures that have produced the most prolific and enduring literature are those in which the people have been well versed in the Word
of God. Bible-influenced cultures have excelled not only in literature

but also in all the other fine arts, sciences, invention, and enterprise. The Word of God has divine power that equips the mind of the child and molds the heart toward greatness. Children educated with a biblical vocabulary and biblical reasoning will become both leaders and contributors to the culture of their community.

Applying this principle in your life

1. Read and sing the Scriptures aloud to your children, beginning at their conception.

2. Set aside a time when the family gathers together and read the children's classics aloud.

3. Have daily family devotions with Bible reading. Teach the meanings of biblical words (Webster's 1828 Dictionary) and passages to your children. (See chapter nine.)

PRINCIPLE 5:
Children communicate and learn not only by words but also through their spiritual eyes and ears

Nonverbal communication is inbuilt by God in our human spirituality.[92] Parents must be attentive to "see" and "hear" what their children are communicating. They need to take note of the child's communication apart from the words he speaks, looking and listening with their spiritual eyes and ears. Likewise, parents must be aware that they are communicating and teaching children by their nonverbal actions. Children easily pick up on the contradiction between what we say and what we do. Their souls take in what their spirits discern about our true values and beliefs from our example. Parents sometimes carry patterns from their own parents of which they may not be consciously aware. Reading and meditating on the Word in our own daily time with the Lord will bring these patterns into conformity with God's nature.

Applying this principle in your life

1. Note areas of inconsistency between your actions and your words. Make God's Word your standard.

2. Observe your child's facial expressions when you are talking with him. Consider what he reveals with his eyes, his tone of voice, and his actions as you "listen" to his spirit and engage with him.

3. Pray for spiritual discernment of your child's spirit, and for spiritual sensitivity and wisdom in your relationship with him.

Closing Thoughts

What have you learned about God's view of children? In what ways does the Christian view of the child differ from what you have believed? All parents will find discrepancies between God's understanding of the nature and value of their child and their own. Now is a good time to acknowledge your need to be transformed by the renewing of your mind in those areas where your view does not agree with the Word of God.

> *Dear Father in Heaven, thank You for showing me through the life of Jesus how dearly You cherish my child. Thank You for entrusting me with the opportunity and responsibility of introducing him to You and raising him to live according to Your ways. Forgive me where I have fallen short and related to my child as the world would. I turn from my culture's view of children and ask that You would alert me where my own views have been shaped by what I have learned from culture. Teach me to see my child as You do. Show me how to raise him according to Your call and purpose for his life. Help me inspire him to accept Christ as His own Savior and Lord. Help me cultivate in my child a love for You and a hunger for Your Word. Instruct me in how to nurture every dimension of my child as one created in Your image. Amen.*

Additional Resources

Adams, Carole G. "The Christian Idea of the Child." *F.A.C.E. Journal, Vol. II*. San Francisco, Calif.: Foundation for American Christian Education, 1991.

Barclay, William. *Educational Ideals in the Ancient World*. Grand Rapids, Mich.: Baker Book House. 1959.

Bunge, M. J., ed. *The Child in Christian Thought*. Grand Rapids, Mich.: Wm. B. Eerdmans, 2001.

Forbes, C. *Imagination: Embracing a Theology of Wonder*. Portland, Ore.: Multnomah Press, 1986.

Glaspey, T. *Children of a Greater God*. Eugene, Ore.: Harvest House Publishers, 1995.

Lindsley, Art. "The Importance of Imagination for C. S. Lewis and for Us." *Knowing & Doing*. C.S. Lewis Institute Report, Summer 2001.

Murray, Andrew. *How to Bring Your Children to Christ*. Springdale:, Pa Whitaker House, 1884.

Stormer, J. *Growing up God's Way*. Florissant, Mo.: Liberty Bell Press, 1984.

Tripp, Ted. *Shepherding a Child's Heart*. Wapwallopen, Pa.: Shepherd Press, 1995.

Weber, H. *Jesus and the children*. Atlanta, Ga.: John Knox Press, 1979.

Wilson, Marvin. *Our Father Abraham: Jewish Roots of the Christian Faith*. Grand Rapids, Mich.: Wm. B. Eerdmans, 1989.

Youmans, Elizabeth. *AMO® Apprenticeship Manual: Principles of Christian Education for Discipling Nations*. Orlando, Fla.: Chrysalis International, 2011.

Youmans, Elizabeth. *The Noah Plan History and Geography Curriculum Guide*. San Francisco, Calif.: Foundation for American Christian Education, 1998.

CHAPTER 7

THE HOME AS A VITAL LEARNING CENTER

God intends for every home to be a vital learning center and every parent a teacher. Home influence is primary and traditional. It transfers the current of life from one generation to the next, especially as it relates to customs and mores, religious values, and the formation of character. Home is the first form of society, a partnership of spiritual and natural life. As a divine institution, it has both a temporal and an eternal mission and, therefore, must provide both physical and spiritual nurture.

> *God intends for every home to be a vital learning center and every parent a teacher.*

Parents are priests to their families and have the divine commission to act for their children as faithful stewards of God in all things pertaining to their temporal and everlasting welfare. As a spiritual nursery, the Christian home is where the foundations of unconditional love, Christian character, and self-government are laid, and where lifelong habits and duties are inculcated. Only in the sphere of Christianity can the true idea of home become fully developed. Sadly, many Christian homes today are corrupted by the influence of the

> **steward** (n.)
> One who cares for the property of another.

habit (n.) A discipline or condition of the mind or body acquired by custom or frequent repetition of the same act. An important aspect of the education of children is to prevent the formation of bad habits.

popular culture and offer little contrast to secular or pagan homes. The knowledge of God is not taught, and parents are content to let the gods of the popular culture disciple their children. Today millions of children in Christian homes spend endless hours being amused and manipulated by non-reflective, media-driven activities that are full of deception and illusion. God issued a strong warning to His people at a time when they, too, had turned their backs on God to worship the gods of their culture:

> *"My people are destroyed for lack of knowledge. Because you have rejected knowledge, I also will reject you from being My priest.* **Since you have forgotten the law of your God, I also will forget your children.***"* (Hosea 4:6, emphasis added.)

God's first call to educate imparted a generational duty to fathers to raise children who know God and obey His precepts

In the Bible, the first call to educate came from the Father-heart of God to the heart of the soon-to-be father Abraham. God's eternal purpose for education is tied to His covenant promise that in Abraham all nations would be blessed (Genesis 17:1–7). Before Isaac was even conceived, God spoke this of Abraham: *"For I have chosen him, in order that he may teach and command his children and his household after him to keep the way of the Lord by doing righteousness and justice, in order that the Lord may bring upon Abraham what He has spoken about him"* (Genesis 18:19).

God placed the primary responsibility for the education of children on fathers. In order for God's covenant blessings to pass through the generations of His chosen people, it was incumbent upon Hebrew fathers to instruct and disciple their children in the precepts and commands of the living, moral God. (Read Deuteronomy 4–6.) **God imparted to Abraham the vision for generational duty by which parents form the future leadership, and indeed the future, through education!** God soon provided the ancient Hebrews with His written Law and ordinances, lest they forget. Knowing

duty (n.) That which a person is bound by moral or legal obligation to pay, do, or perform for another.

and obeying God's precepts and commands consecrated their hearts and minds, protected them from evil, and abundantly prospered them (read Deuteronomy 28)! As guardians and stewards of the next generation, each generation of parents has a divine mandate to "think generationally" and teach Truth to their children for Christian living and leadership.

A biblical, Christian view of education is needed in our nations today

As a divine institution, education's primary purpose is to impart Truth. Therefore, the foundational principle of biblical education is to teach Jesus Christ and His Word. Truth is embodied in Jesus Christ, the living Word of God, and recorded in the Bible, God's handbook for life and living. Education, therefore, is a major arena of the spiritual battle that rages in the world. For this reason, **education is not neutral,** as many Christians believe. Education is a religious function of society that produces the ideals, traditions, and character of the next generation. What an individual believes about God and government forms his worldview of education.

The foundational principle of biblical education is to teach Jesus Christ and His Word.

Education is biblically defined by Noah Webster, father of American Christian education, in his original 1828 *American Dictionary of the English Language,* a one-of-a-kind dictionary in which definitions include biblical meanings:

> The bringing up, as of a child, instruction; formation of manners. Education comprehends all that series of instruction and discipline which is intended to enlighten the understanding, correct the temper, and form the manners and habits of youth, and fit them for usefulness in their future stations. To give children a good education in manners, arts and science, is important; to give them a religious education is indispensable; and an immense responsibility rests on parents and guardians who neglect these duties.

Webster defines education for the whole child and names parents as the primary stewards. Because children are a divine trust, parents are responsible to seek God's will and providence for nurturing each one. Parents are to be actively involved with the spiritual training and character formation of their children, as well as to be cognizant of the content of their academic instruction at every grade level of learning, whether they are the primary instructors or are served by qualified teachers.

Today, most Christians abdicate the instruction and discipline of their children at a very young age to others outside the home—daycare workers, schoolteachers, athletic coaches, Sunday school teachers, youth pastors, and other educational specialists. Sadly, the majority of Christian parents enroll their children in state schools,[93] which overtly teach an anti-Christian belief system and produce a character that is dependent on the state. What is even more alarming is that many teachers in Christian schools have a dualistic mindset and are unable to establish and defend truth in their subjects. The curriculum in many Christian schools imparts the same secular philosophy of education and government as the public school curriculum. May parents repent, turn their hearts back to the hearts of their children, and restore their homes as Christian learning centers.

PRINCIPLE 1:
Parents need vision and a plan to nurture each child for life and leadership

The Old Testament provides inspiration for parents in their role of equipping children for life and leadership. The book of Judges recounts the history of the birth of Samson during an era much like our own, when *"every man did what was right in his own eyes"* (Judges 21:25). The story begins with the visitation of the angel of the Lord, who appeared to the barren wife of Manoah. He told her that she would soon give birth to a son, who would deliver Israel from her enemies. Upon learning that they were to become parents, Manoah prayed, *"O Lord, please let the man of God whom you have sent come to us again that he may teach us what to do for the boy who is to be born . . . [and] what shall be the boy's mode of life and his vocation"* (Judges 13:8; 13). God listened to Manoah's entreaty and returned to give instructions for the boy's call of leadership.

Because Samson was separated unto the Lord, there were certain restrictions that set him apart from other boys in his village. Yet, in obeying God's instructions, Samson grew to fulfill God's purpose in the defeating of the Philistines. The amazing aspect of this account is that the angel, whose name was "Wonderful" (Judges 13:18; Isaiah 9:6), was actually a self-manifestation of God (theophany) or the preincarnate Jesus Christ, who appeared twice to this mother! (Read Judges 13 and be inspired.) **This is the degree of importance that God places on parents to educate and disciple their children for His eternal plan.** This child of promise became a deliverer of his people. Samson was a leader for twenty years who demonstrated great courage and love for the Israelites. His sexual immorality eventually was his undoing, which makes his life a valuable tool for teaching youth the importance of obeying God's Word and possessing moral character.

Like Manoah, you can trust that, if you humbly entreat the Lord for wisdom in raising your children, He will provide not only specific revelation and vision for each individual child but also a practical plan you can follow. God's plan for each child complements the specific internal gifts and talents with which He endows each child in the womb. God graciously provides for each child to attain his full potential and destiny in Christ. (Read Psalm 139.) Equally, each child has a call *"to serve God's purpose in his own generation"* (Acts 13:36). God is generous in His provision for parenting and is always available for the asking to walk with parents. *"Ask, and it will be given to you; seek, and you will find; knock, and it will be opened to you. For everyone who asks receives, and he who seeks finds, and to him who knocks it will be opened"* (Matthew 7:7, 8).

Applying this principle in your life

1. Do you have a vision and an educational plan for each one of your children? If not, pray and ask the Lord to give you a picture of His divine purpose for each child. Like Manoah, ask the Lord to direct you in teaching and discipling each one. Write the vision down and date it. Place it in your Bible and use it when praying for your child and when blessing him.

2. Ask the Lord to show you each child's natural and spiritual abilities and gifts. God endows children in the womb with those faculties that will assist them in fulfilling His calling. As a parent, you will want to intentionally nurture and cultivate those abilities and gifts. That is the essence of the

meaning of Proverbs 22:6: *"Train up a child in the way he should go, even when he is old he will not depart from it."*

3. Provide a lovely setting in your home where the family can spend reflective time together. Build a library of child-appropriate books and resources.

4. Furnish tools for personal study for each child: a Bible, a prayer journal, a binder with paper, colored pencils, a world atlas, etc.

PRINCIPLE 2:
A wholistic, Christian world and life view is needed to nurture children in Christ

Today, many Christians have a dualistic, fragmented world and life view that is rooted in the secular-sacred divide of ancient Greek philosophy. The Greeks divided creation into two self-existing realms and believed that the spiritual realm was superior to the physical realm. Therefore, they considered the invisible part of man pure but the material corrupt. The ancient Hebrew worldview opposes this Greek perspective. The Hebrews viewed man as one whole, created in God's image for His glory. Deuteronomy 6:5 acknowledges God's view of man as an integrated whole: *"You shall love the Lord your God with all your heart and with all your soul and with all your might."* The Hebrews understood that as God's covenant children, they were to be literate and teach God's Law for lifelong, obedient service[94] and holy living. God set

Torah (n.) "Judaism's most important text. It is composed of the Five Books of Moses and also contains the 613 commandments (*mitzvot*) and the Ten Commandments. The word "Torah" means 'to teach.'"[96]

them apart in every dimension of life,[95] so Israel could be a light to the Gentile nations. They believed God chose them for this special task and that the Torah was given to keep them focused on that assignment.

The Hebrew home was the center of education, and both parents shared the responsibility to teach and discipline. They nurtured each child in spirit, soul, and body, integrating all three dimensions in their teaching. God told them to instruct their children while sitting at home, walking along the road, lying down, and rising in the morning.[97] This view of man as an integrated being is reiterated in the New Testament: *"Now may the God of peace Himself sanctify you entirely; and may your **spirit and soul and body** be preserved complete, without blame at the coming of our Lord Jesus Christ"* (1 Thessalonians 5:23, emphasis added).

Child-life was considered particularly holy, and the duty of filling it with thoughts of God especially sacred. The Hebrew mother was the child's first teacher and her smile his first lesson. She nursed her little one for three years and prayed for specific ways to nurture him to fulfill God's purpose for his life. She lit the lamp of his spirit with pure oil and impressed God's Word upon his soul (Exodus 11:18). Each child was given careful memory training before the age of three and taught to read and write before the age of five. It was during this time that she introduced the psalms, the Hebrew songbook, and taught her children God's providential hand in their history. She took seriously her role to impart to her toddler the domestic traditions and festival songs of their Hebrew culture.

The Hebrew father was the child's guardian, protector, and primary instructor of the Torah. For Jews, knowing the Scriptures was their life (Deuteronomy 30:19, 20). The Torah produced the living faith and steadfast character demonstrated by young Daniel and his three Hebrew friends during their Babylonian captivity. Trained early in their lives by their parents in the Law of God, their minds held tenaciously to truth as they were brutally marched from their Jerusalem homes to immoral Babylon, the "Hollywood of the ancient world." Educated in Nebuchadnezzar's Chaldean school of statesmanship, they bravely refused his rich diet and proved their intellectual and spiritual acumen as graduates. Young Daniel was selected not only by the king for national leadership as a prefect in Babylon but also by God as a major prophet to the Jews. These four youths never succumbed to the prevailing world's system or bowed to pagan gods. They stood for the Truth of God's Word in the face of death. They proved to be godly leaders in the midst of a dark civilization and left for us a rich legacy to pass on to our children.

Jesus is a model in the Hebraic tradition of being nurtured as a whole child

There are other inspiring examples of wholistic nurturing in the Bible. It is recorded of young Samuel (1 Samuel 2:26), John the Baptist (Luke

1:80), and Jesus Christ (Luke 2:40, 52) that each one "increased in wisdom and stature, and in favor with God and men." While we do not know the details of Jesus' home life, we do know the outcome: *"Jesus kept increasing in wisdom and stature, and in favor with God and men"* (Luke 2:52). This verse describes four areas in which Jesus grew—intellectually, physically, spiritually, and socially.[98]

At the time of Jesus, young children were first instructed at home by their parents. By the age of six both girls and boys could read and write, and they went on for the next five years to receive a formal education in the synagogue schools with the Jewish Bible as their exclusive textbook! As a result, there is no other nation in history where children were so conscientiously educated as in ancient Israel. There is no reason to think that Jesus was educated in any other way. The description of His childhood development reflects the Hebrew emphasis on nurturing the whole man for time and eternity. Jesus developed His full potential within the context of His Hebrew family. As Mary and Joseph obeyed God's instructions, Jesus was perfectly equipped to fulfill both the Law and the will of His heavenly Father. Jesus received love, provision for his physical body, instruction in the Law and spiritual disciplines, training as a carpenter,[99] discipline to honor and obey his parents,[100] and faith in a relationship with His heavenly Father.[101]

The remarkable life of Susanna Wesley

Parents will also be inspired by the remarkable life of Puritan Susanna Wesley (1669–1743), English mother of John and Charles Wesley. Her legacy of ennobled motherhood remains today an extraordinary model for all Christian parents. Susanna was the twenty-fifth child of noted seventeenth-century scholar and Puritan pastor Dr. Samuel Annesley, at whose knee she received an excellent and classical home education. Susanna described the religious practice she observed growing up:

> I will tell you what rule I observed . . . when I was young and too much addicted to childish diversions, which was this—never to spend more time in mere recreation in one day than I spent in private religious devotions.[102]

Susanna married a Puritan pastor before she reached the age of twenty and gave birth to nineteen children, of whom ten survived infancy. Her devout yet practical manner and her childrearing and educational methods were rooted in her own childhood. Her father saw the family unit as a microcosm of the Church and wrote, "Should not families be as well-ordered little Commonwealths, well-disciplined Churches?" For Susanna this meant firm discipline, spiritual maturity, a good education, and an unselfish concern for the wellbeing of others. Her deep love and concern for the souls of her children and her biblical methods of instruction and discipline nurtured each of her children for a life of Christian leadership. She invested six hours a day in the formal education of her children, which she initiated the day after each child's fifth birthday.

Susanna was often left alone while her husband traveled on church business, yet she governed her well-ordered home with the help of only one servant, homeschooled all her children, and prayed two hours every day. She spent time with each of her children individually and scheduled her undivided attention to one child at a time for one hour each day! Even though she endured much tribulation and financial hardship, she dedicated her life to investing a sense of divine purpose into each of her children. Of the ten Wesley children, their three sons graduated from Oxford University and were ordained by the Church of England. John Wesley, evangelist and church planter, founded Methodism and planted the gospel in the North American English colonies, while his brother, Charles, wrote thousands of poems and hymns still found in church hymnals today.

Despite the limitations on women at that time, Susanna Wesley exercised an independence of conscience as she followed the truths of Scripture. Later in life, when asked by her son John for her rules of raising children, she compiled them in a long letter. Years later, he incorporated her letter into his journal. Her first principle was, "Conquer the child's will and bring it to an obedient temper, because religion is nothing else than doing the will of God and not our own. Self-will is the root of all sin and misery." Susanna Wesley's principles of childrearing and discipline are worthy of our reflection and consideration today. Here is a brief summary:

- Subdue self-will in a child.
- Teach a child to pray as soon as he can speak.
- Do not permit eating between meals.

- While children, they are to be in bed by 8 P.M.

- Require all to be still during family worship.

- Give them nothing that they cry for, and only that when asked for politely.

- To prevent lying, punish no fault that is first confessed and repented of.

- Never allow a sinful act to go unpunished.

- Never punish a child twice for a single offense.

- Comment upon and reward good behavior.

- Any attempt to please, even if poorly performed, should be commended.

- Preserve property rights, even in the smallest matters.

- Strictly fulfill all promises.

- Require no daughter to work before she can read well.

- Teach children to fear the rod.[103]

Susanna believed that for a child to mature as a self-governing adult he must first be a parent-disciplined child. She found that stubborn flesh is the hardest battle for Christians to fight and that Christian parents do well to equip their children to overcome their flesh early in life. From her writing:

> When the will of a child is totally subdued and is brought to revere and stand in awe of his parents, then a great many childish follies may be passed by. I insist on the conquering of the will of children betimes, because this is the only strong and rational foundation of a religious education. When this is thoroughly done, then a child is capable of being governed by reason and piety.[104]

Applying this principle in your life

1. Like Susanna Wesley, routinely intercede for each child. Claim God's promises for him.

2. Teach your child how to pray and keep a prayer journal.

3. Fathers and mothers, make time to be with each child in-
    dividually at least once a week. Write it on your calendar
    and remind each child so they can plan ahead for your
    shared time.

PRINCIPLE 3:
A parent has the responsibility to teach his child the art of self-government

Discipleship also includes teaching the child the knowledge and art
of self-government. Home is the primary sphere of government, in-
volving law, authority, and obedience. The Christian principle of self-
government is God ruling internally from the heart of the believer. For
this to happen, the individual must willingly (voluntarily) submit to
the will or Lordship of Jesus in his life. The only alternative is to be
ruled by external force or law. Government is first internal (causal)
and then extends outward (effect). *"For if a man knows not how to
rule his own house, how shall he take care of the
church of God?"* (1 Timothy 3:5). The New Testament view of leadership and authority teaches
that a man cannot govern well in the civil or
ecclesiastical spheres if he cannot govern well
his family. A man cannot govern well his family

> **government** (n) (1) Control; restraint. (2) The exercise of authority. (3) Direction; regulation.

if he cannot govern himself and submit his thoughts, appetites, and
reason to the Lordship of Jesus Christ and willingly obey Him.

Parents must first teach their children that the source of all authority, law, and government is found in God and defined in His
Word. God delegates His authority to parents, who represent Him as
they govern their homes. When children obey their parents as unto
the Lord, they are ultimately obeying God. Christian self-government
makes God's Law the requirement of the heart (internal). It goes beyond self-discipline or self-restraint because it is motivated by a heart
that loves God and desires to obey His Law. Self-discipline can be
motivated by selfishness or fear of punishment. The more one obeys
the will of God (or His delegated representative) and exercises self-
government, the less external force, law, or government he requires.
The individual must be born again to voluntarily come under the governance of God. When Christ dwells within, He plants the kingdom

of God in our hearts and gives us His Holy Spirit to teach, reveal, and interpret the laws for us (Jeremiah 31:31; Matthew 18:1, 3). Christian self-government requires love, grace, and a lifetime of practice.

Very young children require boundaries and rules for their protection. As they grow, they must be assigned duties and responsibilities and learn how to perform them cheerfully and willingly. Christian self-government is strengthened when children are given opportunities to practice and grow in a loving environment and are commended often. There may be mistakes but, if the lesson is learned in an environment of love, self-government will be strengthened. *"He who is slow to anger is better than the mighty, and he who rules his spirit, than he who captures a city"* (Proverbs 16:32). Christian educator and author James Rose writes,

> Christian self-government in the home does not mean surrendering authority to our children. It does involve delegating authority to a child to accomplish a well-defined task or assignment and expecting a response-ability for the trust or confidence given. Daily opportunities to "be faithful over a few things" and to voluntarily accept authority with responsibility, liberty with law (clearly stated demands or rules of conduct) are necessary to enable a child to become "ruler over many things" (Matthew 25:21).[105]

Christian self-government also involves teaching our children the three functions of government found in the godhead, as recorded in Isaiah 33:11: (1) I plan; (2) I execute; and (3) I evaluate. Children must learn how to steward and manage well their time, their duties, and their internal and external property. They must make plans and develop the habit of assessing the results of carrying them out. As they do, they grow in wisdom, self-governance, and Christian character. Others naturally follow them as they lead by example.

An excellent tool for teaching and practicing Christian self-government in the home is a "family covenant." A covenant or compact is a mutual consent or promise of two or more persons to walk together according to specified terms. Marriage is an example of a covenantal relationship. The terms of agreement are generally written, and the individuals are bound by their signatures to the terms. Covenant is a biblical concept rooted in the very nature of God, who has walked with man since the beginning of time through everlasting covenants. His covenants stipulate the conditions of the relationship and are unchangeable and irrevocable.

Family Covenant

(Insert your family photo.)

We, the parents and children of the _____ family, in order to: (1) form a joyful, well-ordered, and harmonious home environment, (2) establish just rules of conduct, (3) nurture a lifelong love of learning, (4) advance each member's divine call and full potential in Christ, (5) secure the blessings of liberty, and (6) entrust our family legacy to the next generation, do establish this covenant for governing ourselves.

We hereby pledge to do the following:

- ❖ Cheerfully obey God and those in authority
- ❖ Daily seek communion with Christ through spiritual disciplines
- ❖ Uphold Colossians 3:12-25 as our standard of conduct
- ❖ Love unconditionally
- ❖ Respect the individuality and property of others in word and deed
- ❖ Wisely steward my personal property and that shared in common
- ❖ Be kind, honest, and forgiving in all relationships
- ❖ Always defer to others and aim to serve their needs
- ❖ Participate in family activities with grace and gratitude
- ❖ Be hospitable to neighbors and friends

Signatures of parents and children

(Toddlers can stamp their fingerprint.)

A family covenant is written by both parents and children, if they are old enough, and then signed voluntarily by each one in the presence of all. It should be posted somewhere in the home as a reminder and a point of reference. It outlines the standard of righteous conduct rather than publishing a long list of rules to follow. (Remember, every posted rule and its corresponding consequence for disobedience must be enforced.) The covenant appeals to the conscience (the knowledge of right and wrong) and consent of those who signed it (internal), rather than following the letter of the law (external). *The letter kills but the spirit gives life!* Transformation and change begin in the heart with its motives.

consent (n.) The yielding of the mind or will to that which is proposed.

The covenant places the responsibility on each individual to govern himself according to the higher standard of Christ. It serves as a tool of justice and mercy when correction or discipline is needed. The parent appeals to the child's conscience and heart motives, which generally produce remorse and repentance. A sample family covenant is provided for you on page 91.

Applying these principles in your life

1. Write a family covenant. Teach the concepts of the covenant to your children. Review the covenant several times a year to refresh the vision of walking together as a family. Use the covenant to appeal to your child's conscience when disciplining him.

2. Study the Christian principle of self-government together as a family. Research this principle in the Scriptures and identify it in the lives of the characters you study with your children.

Closing Thoughts

Today, Christian parents would be wise to restore the home as a vital, family learning center and to employ a biblical model of raising children in the nurture and admonition of the Lord. It is evident that youth are to be nurtured in intellect and character by early home education and systematic instruction and discipline in biblical principles. Witness, as testimony, the lives of Jesus, Daniel and his friends, and John and Charles Wesley.

Heavenly Father, after reading this chapter and meditating on these principles, I am convicted of the way I relate to my children and the lack of time I spend with them. I ask Your forgiveness and

I repent. I need Your help seeking their forgivingness and in making the necessary changes in my life and my weekly schedule. I desire to see our home as a place of joy and a vital learning center. Give me fresh ideas for interacting with my children. Help us write a family covenant that will transform our lives and the way we relate to one another. Help us rebuild our trust in one another and bless our time of fellowship. In Jesus' name I pray. Amen.

Additional Resources

Balswick, Jack, and Judith Balswick. *The Family: A Christian Perspective on the Contemporary Home.* Grand Rapids, Mich.: Baker Academic, 2007.

Eliot, Elisabeth. *The Shaping of a Christian Family: How My Parents Nurtured My Faith.* Grand Rapids, Mich.: Fleming H. Revell, 1992.

Sandford, John, and Paula Sandford. *Restoring the Christian Family.* Lake Mary, Fla: Charisma House, 2009.

Sisemore, Timothy. *Our Covenant with Kids: Biblical Nurture in Home and Church.* Ross-shire, Great Britain: Christian Focus Publications, 2000.

CHAPTER 8

NURTURING THE WHOLE CHILD
FOR LIFE AND LEADERSHIP

After Jesus was resurrected, He manifested Himself alive for a period of forty days to His apostles and imparted principles of leadership and discipleship for them to follow and teach others. One such occasion took place on the shore of the Sea of Galilee. After asking Peter *"Do you love Me?"* Jesus commanded him to *"Feed My lambs"* (John 21:15). Peter, who would soon become the pastor of the Jerusalem church, was admonished by Jesus to pay particular attention to the nurture of the youngest of his flock—young in following Christ and young in years. The word "feed" contains a wholistic view of Christian discipleship. It means "to nourish the inner man with spiritual food; to provide hope and good expectation; to cherish; to supply the eyes with beauty; to guard and protect; to tend with gentle care; and to lead to good pasture for sustained growth."[106] Peter was a local fisherman instructed as a child in the *letter* of the Law by his father and then in synagogue classes like all other young Jewish boys of his day. The goal was to fulfill the Law. Jesus imparted to Peter the *spirit* of Christian education and discipleship, which He taught and modeled to His apostles through a loving relationship.

In order to nurture and equip the next generation for life and leadership, parents are to instruct each child in the knowledge of God's wisdom and authority through a loving relationship. It is not enough to provide for a child's physical comfort and tell him how to think and what to do. Parents are to lead their child on a pathway of learning about the world around him; about his basic nature and God-given individuality; and about the reality of walking with Jesus Christ, the great, eternal Shepherd. This requires a long-term investment of time, developing a loving, honest relationship with your child through open communication, and consistent discipline in love. Parents are commissioned by God and given authority to lead their children to the green pastures and still waters of beauty, truth, and moral goodness.

lead (v.) To go first and show others the way.

PRINCIPLE 1:
Nurturing a child for life and leadership
begins internally with his heart

Too often, Christian parents focus on their child's external adherence to a list of rules. But following the rules does not transform a rebellious or unbelieving heart! God is interested in cultivating the child's intellect and heart attitudes, so he will grow to love and worship God and practice the art of self-government under the Lordship of Christ. In order to nurture a child's heart for God, the parent must understand the nature of a child. Created in the image of God, man is designed to worship God. By nature, man is essentially religious. From his early years, man worships either God or idols. The heart is the wellspring out of which flow all the issues of life! As Proverbs 4:23 teaches, "*above all else, guard your heart for everything you do flows from it*" (NIV).

Parents must be mindful of the fallen nature of mankind and the basic condition of every child's heart. The heart is not morally neutral. The Bible teaches us how God views the heart of man and what provision He made to redeem it: "*The Lord saw that the wickedness of man was great on the earth, and that every intent of the thoughts of his heart was only evil constantly*" (Genesis 6:5). "*The heart is more deceitful than all else and is desperately sick; who can understand it?*" (Jeremiah 17:9). Man sins because he is a sinner! Children sin and need a Savior. Each child is born with Adam's fallen moral nature (Psalm 51:5; 58:3) and must be taught how to assess himself as a sinner and see his need for forgiveness and redemption. In his book *Shepherding a Child's Heart,* Tedd Tripp states:

> There is no such thing as a place of childhood neutrality. Either your children worship God or idols. These idols are not small statuary. They are the subtle idols of the heart such as conformity to the world, being earthly minded, and setting the affections on things below. . . . The central focus of childrearing is to bring children to a sober assessment of themselves as sinners. They must understand the mercy of God, who offered Christ as a sacrifice for sinners. How is that accomplished? You must address the heart as the fountain of behavior and the conscience as the God-given judge of right and wrong. The cross of Christ must be the central focus of your childrearing.[107]

The heart is the command center of the child's life

In the Hebrew mindset, the heart directs all the faculties of the soul—mind, will, and emotions. *"As a man thinks in his heart, so he is"* (Proverbs 23:7). The heart is where the process of transformation begins, the mind is renewed, and choices are initiated. God designed the heart of man as the command center for governing all of life. The condition of one's heart determines his behavior. Jesus taught, *"the good man out of the good treasure of his heart brings forth what is good; and the evil man out of the evil treasure brings forth what is evil; for his mouth speaks from that which fills his heart"* (Luke 6:45).

The condition of one's heart determines his behavior.

All instruction should aim for the heart. The goal of teaching and learning is to acquire *heart* knowledge, that which motivates and directs a man's actions. Knowing God is the highest form of knowledge and involves the totality of his being, including *worshipping* the Lord and *doing* His will. The command to *"love the Lord your God with all your heart and soul and mind"* (Matthew 22:37) does not point to three distinct dimensions of man but to the totality of his personality. The full nature of the soul remains a mystery but encompasses one vital personality with all its capacities functioning as a whole, as expressed in Psalm 103:1: *"Bless the Lord, Oh my soul, and all that is within me, bless His Holy name."* God has placed capacities or wells of energy within our soul for which we are accountable to subdue, govern, and conform to the full stature of Jesus Christ (Ephesians 4:13).

Our role as parents is to *express* vision and hope for our children and *inspire* them to a living relationship with Jesus Christ. We are accountable to instruct them in knowing and serving God. We must nurture their ability to govern their actions under the Lordship of Christ, while protecting them from physical harm and anti-Christian influences. Parents are the guardians of each child's developing personality. They must routinely survey those influences that shape their child's worldview, tender sensibilities, and imagination by asking: Is he obedient or rebellious? How does he use his free time? What images does my child see every day? What music and conversations is he listening to? What ideals and ideas are promoted in the games he plays, the books he reads, and the organizations he joins? Who are his friends and what standard do his friends' parents uphold in their homes? Who are the role models he interacts with or seeks to emulate? What are their worldview and character? Who are his heroes? Ultimately, who or what is the object of my child's love? Who or what is he worshipping or idolizing?

The life of a child can be compared to an ancient walled city

Throughout history, man protected his cities from enemy assaults by building strong walls around them. Entrance into the city was through heavily guarded gates that were bolted and closed every night and during enemy attacks. High towers were erected on either side of the gates and watchmen were positioned inside. Ancient Jerusalem was no exception. Her walls were constructed with an interior and exterior wall, the distance between the two being so wide that many chariots could ride abreast on top and families could dwell within.

"Like a city that is broken into and without walls is a man who has no control over his spirit." (Proverbs 25:28)

The twelve gates in Jerusalem's walls were literally rooms, each with two wooden doors—one hung on the interior wall and one on the exterior wall. The city elders sat in these gates to administer judicial matters (Deuteronomy 16:18–21; 2 Samuel 15:2; Proverbs 31:23). Scrolls containing God's Law were placed in these rooms, so in the case of disputes the elders consulted God's Word for their decisions. The gates were also civic centers where news was exchanged and goods were traded (Genesis 19:1; Nehemiah 8:1; Isaiah 3:18). Kings sat at the gates to meet with their subjects (2 Samuel 19:8; Jeremiah 38:7), while the Law was read and prophets' admonitions were pronounced there (Joshua 20:4; Nehemiah 8:1, 3; Isaiah 29:21; Jeremiah 17:19). For these reasons, "city gates" are symbolic in the Bible of authority, truth, and protection. While gates were very important as a walled city's first means of defense, they were also extremely vulnerable because they were constructed of wood and easily burned or knocked down.

During the post-exilic period of the Jews' Babylonian captivity, God called Nehemiah, whose name means "comforter," to rebuild Jerusalem. After Nehemiah surveyed the destruction and degeneracy of the city, he initiated a remarkable restoration project by *first* constructing and hanging new wooden gates in the city's walls. The rebuilding of those gates symbolized a work of the Holy Spirit that prepared the Jews for a fresh encounter with God and a renewal of His covenant. Ultimately, God was preparing His chosen people for the coming of His Messiah. A study of the book of Nehemiah and each of the Old City gates provides us with remarkable principles of how to live the victorious Christian life. Just as Nehemiah positioned watchmen in the towers and guards at each of the gates in Jerusalem's wall,[108] so parents must be vigilant as watchmen and guard the vulnerability of our little ones as they grow and mature.

Gates are symbolic in the Bible of authority, truth, and protection.

PRINCIPLE 2:
Parents must guard and nurture the gates to their child's inner man

Using the metaphor of an ancient walled city, envision the education and discipleship of your child as a protective wall that you prayerfully erect around him, with godly wisdom and discernment guarding the gates or entry points to his heart. If you erect a strong defense beginning in infancy and take seriously your divine mandate to nurture your child in the admonition of the Lord when he is young, you will provide the setting in which your child can best grow and mature in God's providence.

NURTURING AND GUARDING THE CHILD'S INNER MAN

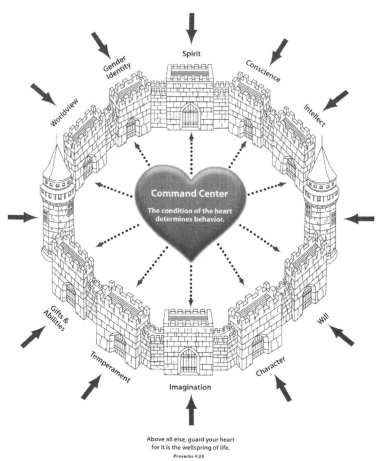

Above all else, guard your heart
for it is the wellspring of life.
Proverbs 4:23

Line upon line, precept upon precept, your child will learn how to refuse evil and choose good (Isaiah 7:14, 15). As he becomes accountable in small things, greater responsibilities can be released for his governance and accountability. He will mature in a loving and forgiving atmosphere where he can experience challenges and triumphs and even make mistakes from which to glean important lessons. He will gradually learn how to trust and worship God with his whole heart, submit his will to that of His heavenly Father, and govern his life responsibly. As God's stewards, parents must intercede and wage the spiritual battle for the hearts and minds of their children; provide life-giving nourishment; and protect against the enemy that comes to rob, steal, and destroy their heritage and covenant blessings.[109]

The Bible is God's inspired and eternal Word. Hebrews 4:12 proclaims, "*God's Word is living and active and sharper than any two-edged sword, and piercing as far as the division of soul and spirit, of both joints and marrow, and able to judge the thoughts and intentions of the heart!*" God's Word is food for man's spiritual growth, as well as a powerful weapon with which to do both offensive and defensive spiritual warfare.

The Bible is also our handbook of Christian principles and practices for application in all of life and leadership. Indeed, God has provided a righteous standard by which to measure and judge cultural influences: "*Whatsoever things are true, whatsoever things are honest, whatsoever things are just, whatsoever things are pure, whatsoever things are lovely, whatsoever things are of good report; if there be any virtue, and if there be any praise, think on these things*" (Philippians 4:8 KJV). God has in fact provided everything we need to nurture our children and has promised He will walk with us and show us the way if we ask Him.

Gate one: Your Child's Spirit

God is Spirit (John 4:24; 2 Corinthians 3:17), and He fashioned man in His own likeness. Man's spirit is that eternal dimension or "*the hidden person of the heart*" (1 Peter 3:4) through which we relate to God. The Hebrew word for "spirit" is most often translated "breath, life, or soul." At creation, God breathed His breath into Adam and man became a living, eternal soul.[110] Then spiritual death resulted from Adam and Eve's sin, and man's relationship with God was broken (Genesis 2:17). But through faith in Jesus Christ, a person's spirit can be converted or born again and restored to full relationship with God in Christ. Jesus taught that "*unless one is born of water and the Spirit he cannot enter into the kingdom of God*" (John 3:5). It is certainly true that the spirit of a young child can be born again. Parents must be watchful and sensitive to the leading of the Holy Spirit for opportune moments to share this precious gift of eternal life with their children. It is through the regenerated spirit that God's Holy Spirit speaks inwardly to the Christian, confirms His love, illumines his understanding, reveals truth, and witnesses to his adoption as a child of God.[111]

Parents must guard this gate with sensitivity, as a child's spirit is tender and easily wounded. Parents cannot prevent every wound, but they should pray with the child for healing and teach the child his part in the healing process. Joy in relationship with God and family members strengthens and gives the spirit resiliency. *"A joyful heart is good medicine, but a broken spirit dries up the bones"* (Proverbs 17:22). If this gate is not guarded until the child's spirit is born again and he is able to govern his own spirit, the child is vulnerable to every idol and form of evil and destruction.

Guarding your child's spirit gate

1. Two steps in guarding your child's spirit are most important: (1) Teach your child the nature of God and the nature of man. Children need to understand what sin is and what to do when they sin. (2) Teach him about Jesus Christ and lead him to Christ as his personal Savior and Lord *(How to Bring Your Children to Christ* by Andrew Murray is a classic resource.[112])

2. Nurture your child's spirit by teaching him how to: (1) worship God with his whole heart and enjoy family fellowship (family worship led by parents is described in chapter nine); (2) maintain a prayer relationship with God; and (3) develop the daily habit of Bible reading.

3. Relate to your child in love with honesty, tenderness, and discernment. Teach him to ask for forgiveness when he sins against others. When he is hurt, deceived, or dealt with unjustly, teach him to bless his enemies and pray for them.[113]

Gate two: Your Child's Conscience

Conscience is the God-given capacity to know right from wrong. It is the first door into the human soul and acts as a security system to keep intruders out and protect righteousness within. It assists the will in making moral decisions. A child's conscience is strengthened when he heeds its witness, obeys God and those in authority over him, and learns biblical doctrine (Hebrews 5:14). The conscience is weakened or hardened when it is ignored. A seared conscience loses its power to guide and convict of poor moral choices. A child who is quick to repent of sin and receive cleansing will keep his conscience pure and effective. Parents need to teach their children how to discern the spirit of truth and the spirit of error (1 John 4:6) and how to refuse evil and choose good (Isaiah 7:15) in spite of the adverse influences around them. This will help the young child maintain a pure conscience as he grows older.

Guarding your child's conscience gate

1. Explain the role of conscience to your child. Teach him how to keep his conscience pure, and what happens when he ignores it.

2. Cultivate your child's inner convictions. Focusing on behavior alone produces hypocrisy and legalism, while it inhibits growth in self-awareness and self-governance. Teach him discernment and how to evaluate the leading of his conscience in the light of God's Word.

3. Teach your child that God's Word is the ultimate standard of good and evil, right and wrong, wisdom and folly. The book of Proverbs is the place to begin instructing children in moral goodness and intellectual rectitude.

   rectitude (n.) Rightness of principle or practice; exact conformity to truth or the rules prescribed for moral conduct; uprightness; integrity; honesty; justice.

4. Teach your child how to hear God's voice, especially when praying and reading the Bible. Practice the presence of God in family prayer. Teach your child how to distinguish God's voice from that of self or Satan.

Gate three: Your Child's Intellect

The intellect is man's mental capacity to think and reason abstractly, by which he *knows* or *understands*, as distinguished from that which he *feels* with his emotions. Scripture teaches us that the unbeliever's mind is easily deceived and blinded by the god of this world (2 Corinthians 11:3; 4:4). The unbeliever walks in the futility of his mind (Ephesians

4:17), and children are vulnerable to such futility and foolishness and easily led astray. Parents are a child's first source of wisdom and understanding and are to guard their child from foolish thinking and perilous actions while his intellect and judgment are being formed. Parents should take every opportunity to teach their child how to think and reason with the revelation of God's Word and to apply truth to his life.

Children must be instructed in moral principles. They need a biblical base of knowledge and a rich vocabulary with which to think and reason. Words are the building blocks of ideas. Teaching and learning by principles, rather than the pursuit of information or the memorization of rules, is an effective manner by which to strengthen a child's intellectual rectitude. It lays the foundation for understanding truth rather than accumulating facts.

principle (n.) (1) The cause, source, or origin of anything; that from which a thing proceeds. (2) Foundation. (3) A general truth or law.

A principle is an absolute truth, a seed. A seed contains everything within its casing to reproduce itself, given the right conditions. Teaching by principles inculcates the habit of reasoning from cause to effect and enables the child to apply truth to a topic or area of study.

Proverbs repeatedly exhorts us to *"Acquire wisdom! Acquire understanding! Do not forget nor turn away from the words of my mouth. Do not forsake her, and she will guard you; love her and she will watch over you"* (Proverbs 4:5–6). Wisdom and understanding come from knowing God.[114] Knowing God is the very purpose of understanding.[115] God gives wisdom and understanding by illumining the individual's intellect, thinking, and reasoning.[116] We see a clear example of this in the lives of Daniel and his Hebrew friends. They showed "intelligence in every branch of wisdom" and were "endowed with understanding and discerning knowledge,"[117] and Daniel was able to understand "all visions and dreams."[118] As the child's mind is renewed by the Word of God, he is transformed into one who thinks with the mind of Christ, one who can lead others based on God's perspective and wisdom.

Guarding your child's intellect gate

1. Intentionally train your child to think and reason with the revelation of truth. Discuss ways in which God's reasoning is different from the world's. Seize every teachable

moment to highlight godly wisdom in choices and conduct. Train your child to see that choices (cause) have consequences (effect).

2. During family Bible readings, ask your child to identify what God is saying and have him reason and apply this understanding to his own life.

3. Help your child learn how to search the Scriptures for God's principles related to situations for which he needs wisdom and for truth to undergird his academic assignments.

Gate four: Your Child's Will

The human will is man's capacity to make choices that govern his conduct. The will is often compared to the rudder of a ship, which directs the ship's course at sea. The will does not operate alone but is subject to powerful influences that are brought to bear upon it. It can be informed by the logic of reason, one's changeable emotions, or the whisper of the tempter or the Holy Spirit. The will's action is determined by the condition of the mind, which, in turn, is influenced by God, the world, the flesh, or the devil. The will must be trained to seek truth and godly wisdom before acting, which requires a lifetime of growing and maturing in Christ.

Much of parenting involves the interaction of the parent's will with that of the child. The goal of the parent is to equip the child in comprehending the fallen nature of his own heart and discovering the blessings of choosing God's will over his own. Sadly, many Christian parents never teach their child how to assess himself as a sinner and seek God's mercy and forgiveness for his sin. God gave parents the responsibility for moral instruction. Children must be faithfully taught God's ways, gently nurtured, and consistently disciplined and corrected.

A child should be taught early to obey his parents. Parents represent God and His authority in the family, and their authority is God-delegated. When a child disobeys his parents, he must be disciplined. Consistency is essential for the formation of a will that glorifies God.

The training process is a delicate balance between providing the greatest possible liberty to and respect for the child and requiring prompt and voluntary obedience. Such obedience from the very young child is not contingent on understanding his parent's reasons. The habit of obeying those in authority prepares the way for readiness to obey God Himself.

Disobedience is rooted in the condition of the heart. Proverbs teaches us that fathers are to discipline the child at a tender age "while there is hope," when the child's habits are being formed. While a "no," a look of disapproval, or a consequence for disobedience is often adequate, spankings are in order for serious violations. *"He who withholds his rod hates his son, but he who loves him disciplines him diligently"* (Proverbs 13:24). All punishment is to be given in love, not in anger.

Tedd Tripp's book *Shepherding a Child's Heart* is an excellent and thorough resource on godly correction. The child may be required to ask for and receive his parents' forgiveness for disobedience. Reconciliation must follow discipline. Always take time to rebuild your relationship with your child after correction. Pray with him. Reassure him of your unconditional love with a hug and kiss. Biblical discipline should earn respect, not provoke anger or engender bitterness.[119] The purpose of disciplining the child's will is for the child's good, so that he may share in God's holiness.[120] *"All discipline for the moment seems not to be joyful, but sorrowful; yet to those who have been trained by it, afterwards it yields the peaceful fruit of righteousness"* (Hebrews 12:11).

Guarding your child's will gate

1. Be strengthened in your own faith concerning God's commission to you as teachers and guardians of your child's personhood! Do not abdicate that responsibility to others. Do not accept the culture's norm as your standard for your child.

2. Covenant with God to raise your child in the nurture and admonition of the Lord.

3. Discipline and correct your child promptly and consistently without anger. It is important that correction be in

private. Discipline often requires the child asking forgiveness and reconciling with another. There may be other consequences as well. Always follow discipline with a hug, a smile, warmth, and reassurance that your love for the child is unconditional.

Gate five: Your Child's Character

Character is the capstone of education, and the family is the nursery of character formation. Character is defined as "the peculiar qualities, impressed by nature or habit on a person, which distinguish him from others."[121] Nineteenth-century English educator Hannah More wrote the following about character formation:

> The formation of character is the grand object to be accomplished in education. This should be considered to be not so much a separate business, but the center to which all the rays of instruction are directed. . . . All intellectual attainments should support the dignity of character, as knowledge is the preservative of virtue. Providence has plainly indicated childhood to be the season of instruction, and parents are bound to convert the impressibility of the heart to its most exalted moral use.[122]

Our character is not a gift from God or inherited from our parents. Our character begins to form in early childhood from personal choices and repeated actions, until those actions become habits (Deuteronomy 28:2, 15; Joshua 24:15; 1 Samuel 15:22; Hebrews 5:8; Luke 22:41, 42). Choices and habits can either be virtuous or foolish and have consequences that lead to life or death.

Parents are the child's first teachers and models of character, those whom the child will imitate from a very early age. Example plays an important part in the formation of the child's character. The influence of example is felt more than that of precept. Christian parents are appointed by God to instruct their young child in the knowledge and authority of God's Word and to train their child to obey God's commands. Jesus taught us that *"a pupil is not above his teacher, but everyone, after he has been fully trained will be like his teacher"* (Luke 6:40). The Bible is our "character handbook" and provides the unchangeable standard for character formation and self-government.

> *And that from childhood you have known the sacred writings which are able to give you the wisdom that leads to salvation through faith which is in Christ Jesus. All scripture is inspired by God and profitable for teaching, for reproof, for correction, **for training in righteousness**; so that the man of God may be adequate, equipped for every good work (2 Timothy 3:15–17, emphasis added).*

Christian character formation begins with knowing Jesus Christ and being strengthened by the indwelling of His Spirit. The child's heart must be transformed and the process of renewing his mind initiated before he can voluntarily submit his will to God's will (1 Peter 1:23; Ephesians 3:16; 1 Thessalonians 1:5; Romans 12:2; Isaiah 1:19). Righteousness is not just what we do or say but how we govern our heart. The Greek word *charakter* in the New Testament is translated "express image." In Hebrews 1:3, Christ is referred to as the "express image" of God. He is the perfect model of God's nature and character. God predestined all Christians to be conformed to the image of His Son and empowers us by the indwelling of His Spirit to become partakers of His divine nature:

> *Grace and peace be multiplied to you in the knowledge of God and of Jesus our Lord; seeing that His divine power has granted to us everything pertaining to life and godliness, through the true knowledge of Him who called us by His own glory and excellence. For by these He has granted to us His precious and magnificent promises, so that by them you may become **partakers of the divine nature**, having escaped the corruption that is in the world by lust. Now for this very reason also, applying all **diligence**, in your faith supply **moral excellence**, and in your moral excellence, **knowledge**, and in your knowledge, **self-control**, and in your self-control, **perseverance**, and in your perseverance, **godliness**, and in your godliness, **brotherly kindness**, and in your brotherly kindness, **love**. For if these qualities are yours and are increasing, they render you neither useless nor unfruitful in the true knowledge of our Lord Jesus Christ (2 Peter 1:2–8, emphasis added).*

Christian character is refined by fiery ordeals and pressure, both within and without (John 15:2, 4; Philippians 1:27; 1 Peter 5:8–10; Hebrews 5:8). God often tries or proves the character of His people through tribulation and pain, as well as conflict with the world and the powers of darkness (1 Peter 4:12, 13; James 1:2, 3; Isaiah 43:1, 2; Zechariah 13:9; Psalm 7:9; Job 23:10; Luke 22:31, 32). He uses suffering and duress to purify our motives, as gold is refined by fire. The Apostle Paul taught *"that tribulation brings about perseverance and perseverance, **proven character;** and proven character, hope; and hope does not disappoint, because the love of God has been poured out within our hearts through the Holy Spirit who was given to us"* (Romans 5:3–5, emphasis added).

One who consciously chooses to obey God experiences hope, and the witness of God's love guards his heart. Parents often shield their children from God's testings and thereby prevent the character growth desired by God. The deceptive lure of fleeting delights easily captures a young child's attention. Scripture warns that Christian character must be free of temporal loves and fears and rest contentedly in God's provision.[123] As children see parents living this way, they grow to desire and imitate those character traits that bring peace and joy.

Christian character is formed from the inside out. As the believer develops the habit of godly choices, he discovers for himself that he does not need to be controlled by sin, nor is he a victim of his environment. He learns to be an overcomer in Christ, through whom all things are possible (Philippians 4:13). Children need to see their parents' response to tribulation and suffering, so they can trust God with their own problems and hardships and learn how to walk through them without losing their faith.

The Bible contains many accounts of individuals who persevered in times of tribulation and suffering, such as Joseph, Moses, Job, David, Daniel and his friends, Esther, Paul, and Jesus, to name a few. Their lives are worthy of study, reflection, and imitation. Children should also be introduced to the lives of other historic models of Christian character by reading biographies of great men and women and time-tested, children's classics such as *Heidi, Hans Brinker or the Silver Skates, Pilgrim's Progress, Charlotte's Web,* and scores of others.

Christian character is never formed in solitude but in community: family, friends, neighbors, those at school or in church, in our job, and in the clubs or organizations we join. *"As iron sharpens iron, so one man sharpens the character of his friend"* (Proverbs 27:17). In addition, the wise parent teaches his children the rules of civility and sociability and requires the practice of them in the home.

Guarding your child's character gate

1. The fruits of the Spirit in your own life are irreplaceable as models and guards for the development of Christian character in your child. Your child will see the result of your conduct and imitate your faith.[124]

2. Complete a thorough study of "God's One Anothers" from the New Testament in your family devotions. See the list of One Anothers in Appendix III. Select one command and highlight it for a month in your home. Display it prominently where the family gathers. Challenge each family member to find a way every week to fulfill the command and to be accountable to the rest of the family by sharing his experience. Discuss how your study of One Anothers affects your perception of others and challenges your own character and heart motives.

3. As a family, study each of the following scriptural passages relating to character in your family devotions. Also, memorize them together.
    > The Ten Commandments (Exodus 20:1–17)
    > Christ's Great Commandment (John 13:34)
    > Christ-like qualities (2 Peter 1:2–11)
    > The Beatitudes (Matthew 5:3–12)
    > The two Great Laws (Matthew 22:36–40)
    > Holy living (Colossians 3:12–17)
    > Obedience to parents (Colossians 3:20; Ephesians 6:1–3)

4. During family devotions, study and discuss the role of character in fulfilling God's purpose and in blessing others. Compare the world's characteristics of greatness with biblical characteristics of greatness.[125] Study the character of biblical figures. Consider traits such as diligence, flexibility, alertness, availability, endurance, hospitality, and

generosity. *Character Sketches* by the Institute in Basic Life Principles[126] is an excellent church library resource.

5. During times of family reading aloud, take time to analyze the character qualities of the characters in the stories being read. The AMO® Program literature guides provide character studies and questions for children to reflect upon as they apply truth to their own lives. (They are available in English, Spanish, and Portuguese.)

6. Recognize your child's tribulations as opportunities to mature. Encourage him, pray for him, and share the wisdom of God's Word as he passes through trials. Affirm your confidence in his ability to walk according to the Spirit and celebrate his successes!

7. Have your children compose character studies of their grandparents or great-grandparents. Suggest that they interview them and then write and illustrate a small biography. Encourage them to describe how their forbears grew up and the influences and experiences that helped form their character. Have them highlight the legacy they have received from them.

Gate six: Your Child's Imagination and Aesthetic Sensibilities

Sadly, there is little teaching that comes from the Church on nurturing Christian imagination in children. Many Christians are ignorant of this God-given faculty and believe the imagination has only to do with dark magic and demonic influences. Yet we all imagine! Understanding the imagination as God purposed for man's ennoblement and creativity begins with a biblical view of God and creation. God created man, the crowning glory of His creation, in His image and endowed him with various faculties that set man apart from the animal kingdom. Those faculties include language, reason, conscience, and imagination. The imagination is that faculty that forms images in the mind and enables creative expression. The imagination has been called "God's gift of wonder."[127] The highest exercise of our imagination is the reverent response of wonder, as we behold His beauty, majesty, and glory and are changed into His likeness.[128] God promises us, *"Thou wilt keep him in perfect peace whose **imagination is stayed on Thee**"* (Isaiah 26:3 RV, 1885, emphasis added).

In general, most Christian parents and youth leaders are content to let the popular culture disciple children's aesthetic sensibilities. As the culture grows darker and children spend endless hours being entertained by media-driven activities, their imaginations become dulled, starved, and corrupted. Today, children are bombarded with hundreds of visual images every day, many of which are immoral, defiled, and even demonic. These images and subliminal messages entertain and defile rather than inspire and dignify children. In many cases, television programs, movies, and games created for children are full of deceptive wonder and illusion rather than truth and reality.

aesthetic (adj.) Pertaining to the nature and principles of beauty.

sensibility (n.) The capacity for feeling or perceiving impressions.

The time to cultivate the Christian imagination is early childhood. Very young children have a natural sense of wonder and a spiritual thirst for beauty and truth. Their minds and hearts are malleable and their memories tenacious. Parents need to capture and hold the child's imagination with Christian ideals, themes, and images before he is old enough to accept the culture's lie that he is *entitled* to view and hear whatever he desires. For these reasons, both the home and the church need to restore their roles in displaying and nurturing truth and beauty in the culture and intentionally guard children's imaginations with images and ideals of magnificence.

One way to cultivate Christian imagination is to nourish it with stories and imagery from the Bible; classic literature and poetry; and the fine and performing arts, such as music, drama, art, dance, and film. When parents read stories aloud to their children, many things happen. First, the child's heart and mind bond to the parent reading the story. The child learns to sit still and listen with his inner ear. Listening is a skill that has to be taught. The child learns to reflect upon the story's theme, plot, and noble characters and let his imagination enter the story. Learning to listen paves the way for a reflective life and hearing the voice of God.

Classic literature and the arts are powerful tools that transcend the mediocre and ugly sphere of our pop culture. The classics, with their

Christian ideals and universal ideas, cultivate the imagination and inspire greatness in children. Combined with reading God's Word, the spiritual potential of children is nourished, and they determine to pattern their own lives after the heroes and heroines they meet. Unlike the digital toys of modernity, the classics and the arts help nurture Christian imagination and truly inspire children to dream God-sized dreams and aspire to live a nobler life.

> The imagination is not neutral! Unless parents, pastors, and teachers *intentionally* choose to cultivate Christian imagination in children, Satan will feed them his deceptive and ugly fare, which is addictive!

The imagination is not neutral! Unless parents, pastors, and teachers *intentionally* choose to cultivate Christian imagination in children, Satan will feed them his deceptive and ugly fare, which is addictive! God has provided us the model of beauty, truth, and moral goodness in His creation and the standard by which to nourish our family's imagination in Philippians 4:8, 9:

> *Whatsoever things are true, whatsoever things are honest, whatsoever things are just, whatsoever things are pure, whatsoever things are lovely, whatsoever things are of good report; if there be any virtue, and if there be any praise, think on these things. Those things, which ye have both learned, and received, and heard, and seen in me, do: and the God of peace shall be with you.* (KJV)

Guarding your child's gate of imagination

1. Parents must be proactive and schedule time to cultivate and nurture Christian imagination. *Doing nothing is not an option.* Begin with a family study of Philippians 4:8, 9. Define the key words in Webster's 1828 Dictionary, which contains biblical definitions and is found online at http://www.1828.mshaffer.com. Providing children with the biblical vocabulary of aesthetics builds fresh ideas. Words are the building blocks of ideas.

2. Practice applying Philippians 4:8 to aesthetic decisions in your home. Teach your children how to discern beauty, truth, and moral goodness in nature, music, art, film, drama, books, and media. Begin with outdoor nature walks.

3. Like Nehemiah, who surveyed the decay and destruction of Jerusalem, *survey your home* and determine where televisions and computers are located. Be cautious about giving your children unsupervised access to these electronic devices in their bedrooms or during free time. Listen to the music that plays in your home and automobile, observe the television programs and movies that are viewed, the artwork or posters on the walls, the use of the internet on computers, and the reading material that lies around. *Pornography is a huge problem in the Body of Christ.* Decide how much time and which television programs and movies you will permit your child to watch. If a parent or responsible adult cannot monitor the television and computer, they should not be accessible to the child. There is no practical way to monitor texting and internet access through cell phones, so these features should be completely disabled on cell phones. Many parents require their children to turn over their cell phones at night to be monitored and charged.

4. From infancy, read aloud a portion of Scripture every day or night to your children. Feed your child's imagination with biblical imagery and symbolism. Read and enact the AMO *Wellspring of Wonder®* program using wooden story figures and colorful underlays.

5. Have a "family reading aloud" schedule in your home. Read the great, universal classics aloud to your children, works such as *Charlotte's Web*, *Hans Brinker*, *Heidi*, the Little House series, *Wind in the Willows*, *Pilgrim's Progress*, *Pinocchio*, and the Narnia books. The AMO® Program has teacher guides for many children's classics for parents to use, available in English, Spanish, and Portuguese (http://www.amoprogram.com). Summer vacation is a great time to select a classic for study. See Additional Resources at the end of this chapter.

6. Create a home library and furnish it with the works of Christian authors like George MacDonald, C. S. Lewis,

G. K. Chesterton, J. R. R. Tolkien, Edmund Spenser, John Milton, and many others.

7. Teach your child's inner eye how to assess beauty in his environment. Adorn your home with images of beauty through flower arrangements, paintings and sculpture, and books on artists and architects. Visit local libraries and museums often. Teach your children how to sketch, paint, and sculpt at an early age, or provide art lessons with a local artist. Take sketchpads and watercolors with you on your nature walks. Frame your children's artwork and display it in your home.

8. Cultivate your children's sensibilities through a variety of music in your home. Include the great classic music of Western civilization. Teach your children how to read music. Provide lessons for them to learn how to play a musical instrument or to dance. Encourage children to join the school chorus, band, or orchestra. When possible, attend theater productions, concerts, and ballets as a family.

9. Plan field studies or family vacations to include visits to museums, theaters, puppet shows, concerts, ballets, operas, and art festivals. Always encourage your children to *express their own imagination* by responding to biblical story, music, and literature with painting, drawing, modeling with clay, dance, or play acting.

Gate seven: Your Child's Temperament

Temperament refers to the God-given characteristics and aspects of an individual's personality. The Hebrew understanding of temperament includes characteristics like vivacity, vigor, patience, and contentment. *"For we are His workmanship, created in Christ Jesus for good works"* (Ephesians 2:10a). Every child needs to learn to submit his temperament to the Holy Spirit and govern it according to Christian standards of character. Children have amazing diversity from birth. Some are even-tempered, regular sleepers, and good feeders. At the other extreme are babies who are fussy, colicky, and seem to struggle with everything. Other differences of temperament include qualities like "activity level, regularity, approach or withdrawal, adaptability, threshold of responsiveness, intensity of reaction, quality of mood, distractibility, attention span, and persistence."[129]

A child's temperament will be shaped, for better or for worse, by his parents. When parents lovingly and carefully govern and nurture the child, he learns to use his strengths and weaknesses for God's glory. God endows every child with unique qualities for specific purposes. These are assets to be harnessed and channeled according to God's divine calling. Often, those temperamental qualities that parents find most frustrating will ultimately become most helpful in fulfilling the "works that God has prepared for"[130] him. Every weakness can be redeemed. Stubbornness can be harnessed for building perseverance and persistence. Impulsiveness in the Apostle Peter became boldness and courage. If we disregard the temperamental qualities of our child instead of helping him use those qualities for God's glory, we will miss the opportunity to nurture his full potential. On the other hand, parents must not tolerate sinful excesses of temperament; thus the New Testament's exhortation to be "temperate."[131]

Guarding your child's temperament gate

1. Give thanks for your child's unique combination of temperament qualities. Call forth his full potential.

2. Become a student of each of your children. Be aware of how each child interacts with people and manages experiences. Consider his individuality as you nurture and teach him. Each child learns and responds best in his own way.

3. Be aware of the kinds of situations in which your child is especially challenged. Some children cannot tolerate a great deal of activity or sensory input. Too many choices easily overload others. Most children thrive on a regular daily schedule, but some children absolutely require it to function.

4. Pray that God will harness all of your child's temperament qualities for His purpose, and that He will give

you wisdom in managing and shaping these qualities for God's purposes.

Gate eight: Your Child's Natural and Spiritual Gifts and Abilities

The Hebrew word for "ability" refers to strength or power in intelligence, understanding, and knowledge. Daniel and his friends are described in Scripture as having *"ability for serving in the king's court."*[132] The Hebrew word for "skill" refers to practical knowledge. It can include natural endowments in thinking, imagination, insight, wisdom, and perception. God endows individuals with skills for all kinds of service: e.g., spinning, weaving, making garments, engraving, designing, metal-working, masonry, carpentry, inventing, writing, hunting, and making war. God *"made the heavens with skill,"*[133] and He gives each person skills to do that which fulfills His eternal plan and brings glory to His name.

Hebrew fathers taught their sons a skill, craft, or trade for making a living. As seen in the life of Jesus, who learned carpentry from his father, a son was apprenticed to his father.[134] Hebrew mothers instructed their daughters in the skills of weaving, garment making, cooking, and management of the home, field, and business.[135] Sons and daughters learned how to play musical instruments and dance.[136] The role of Christian parents is to recognize the child's skills and provide instruction to master those skills for successful living. A child's aptitudes are internal property given by God for use in His kingdom, to provide for family and community.

Spiritual gifts are supernatural endowments given by God to serve one another according to God's purposes. God gives every believer at least one spiritual gift, enabling him to fulfill his divine calling. *"The gifts and the calling of God are irrevocable"* (Romans 11:29). Spiritual gifts are often (but not always) divorced from natural traits. Moses stuttered and was naturally insecure about his speaking ability, yet God called and gifted him to confront Pharaoh. Spiritual gifts enable a person to do things that in his own natural strength or ability would be impossible. *"We have this treasure in earthen vessels, so that the surpassing greatness of the power will be of God and not from ourselves"* (2 Corinthians 4:7).

Since the advent of the Holy Spirit, spiritual gifts are given to all Christians for the building up of the Body of Christ. Read 1 Corinthians 12. The New Testament identifies spiritual gifts as *"prophecy, service, teaching, exhortation, giving, leading, and mercy"* (Romans 12:3–8), *"word of wisdom, word of knowledge, faith, gifts of healing, miracles, prophecy, distinguishing of spirits, various kinds of tongues, interpretation of tongues, helps, and administrations"* (1 Corinthians 12:4–11, 28). Spiritual gifts are given for *"the common good."*[137] When we serve others in love, our gifts are manifested and confirmed. If a young child is given instruction and oversight, he readily learns to use the gifts God has given him.

Like other internal property of the child, spiritual gifts need to be stewarded by the parent in his early years. *"As each one has received a special gift, employ it in serving one another as good stewards of the manifold grace of God"* (1 Peter 4:10). The child must learn how to use his gifts in the context of an intimate relationship with God, based on the Word and prayer. Without love, the gifts are meaningless;[138] thus Christian character must be cultivated as the foundation for ministry. Children need to be taught to desire and seek spiritual gifts for the edification of the Church, not for their own honor or glory.[139] Children are able to experience the supernatural. However, some turn to evil and occult games, books, and practices because they have never encountered the true power of God. Children need to be taught the difference between true and counterfeit gifting.

Guarding your child's natural and spiritual gifts and talents gate

1. Guard your child from cartoons and preschool television programs of evil beings; from popular books, games, and movies about the supernatural; and from the plethora of TV programs that illustrate the practice of demonic power and witchcraft.

2. Take your child with you when you minister to others, e.g., when you go to help a neighbor or pray for someone who is sick. Bring your child up in an atmosphere of serving and helping others so that they can experience the power of God firsthand.

3. Take note of how your family and others respond to the loving service of your child. Help your child begin to identify the special ways in which God has gifted him.

4. Teach your child basic skills. Consider members of your extended family and church for help. Plan time in your family's calendar for teaching these skills as an enjoyable activity.

5. Provide opportunities for your child to meet people in your community who are especially skilled in various areas. This will enable him to become aware of his own interests and to develop vision for how his abilities can be used for God's glory and to serve others.

6. Be alert for the unique aptitudes that your child exhibits so that you can encourage him and give special instruction to him in those particular skills and abilities. Your role is to help your child discover and steward his God-endowed individuality, not to shape and mold him after yourself.

Gate nine: Your Child's Worldview

Today's culture war is a clash between the competing worldviews of truth and falsehood. The battleground is the hearts and minds of children. Worldview is the mindset from which we see the world and live our lives. It is rooted in our basic beliefs about the nature of reality. The daily choices we make are determined by our worldview. Our worldview answers questions like: "What is the purpose of life?" "Is there a God?" "If there is a God, how does He relate to the world?" Effective childrearing depends on teaching our children to see all of life through a biblical lens. Knowledge of the Bible is essential for every child. They also need a broader framework connecting their spiritual beliefs to their overall vision of reality. Pollster George Barna stated, "Without a biblical worldview, all great teaching goes in one ear and out the other. There are no intellectual pegs . . . in the mind of the individual to hang these truths on, so they just pass through. They don't stick. They don't make a difference."[140]

Studies by the Nehemiah Institute conclude, "At least 90 percent of youth from Christian homes attend either public schools or traditional Christian schools and consistently abandon the Christian worldview in favor of the humanist/socialist worldview."[141] The Bible presents the only objective and completely true worldview. Every other worldview is a distortion of truth that occurs as a result of the Fall of man. Chapter one of this book examined the impact of worldview. Accordingly, it is vital to develop a biblical, Christian worldview in children. The culture's secular worldview will impact their thinking if parents, teachers, and pastors do not *intentionally nurture* their minds with the Word of God[142] and teach them how to apply its truths to all of life! Pastor Voddie Baucham warns, "If we do not give our children a biblical worldview, they will simply follow our rules while they are under our watchful eye, but as soon as they gain independence, they will make decisions based upon their worldview."[143]

idea (n.) (1) A thought or conception that exists in the mind as the product of mental activity. (2) An opinion, conviction, or principle.

An adult, by exercising his will, shapes his culture. In the same way, a child directs the course of his life. That direction comes from ideas. His future is not determined by his external environment, but by his *internal beliefs and choices*. "*As he thinks within himself, so he is*" (Proverbs 23:7). The human mind is susceptible to suggestive ideas, especially in childhood. Therefore, parents and teachers must teach the ideas that will build a biblical worldview beginning in early childhood and guard against secular humanism. Over time, this process builds mental models of God, self, and reality that provide the child a powerful grid through which to filter cultural values and ideals purported by their peers, teachers, textbooks, and the media and to discern deception and illusion.

Guarding your child's worldview gate

1. Identify the sources of a secular worldview in your home and community. Screen television programs, DVDs, CDs, internet sites, and social networks. Scan your children's textbooks. Inquire every day what they are learning in their classes. Keep family discussions alive and detoxify when necessary. Keep abreast of your children's assignments and required classes. Take action at school or with

the school board when they conflict with your biblical standard.

2. The power of persuasion is compelling. Discuss the hidden worldview and subliminal messages of advertisements. Children are major consumers who are heavily targeted by advertisement campaigns. (In the United States, over $12 billion per year is spent on children.) Help your children uncover the lies and deception promoted through commercials and marketing ploys.

3. Instruct your child in biblical doctrine while he is young, and build upon it as he matures. The first-century Church developed an oral form of catechism for children,[144] and for over 450 years, the Reformed Church has employed a catechism such as the *Genevan Catechism, the Westminster Catechism, and the Heidelberg Catechism*. A catechism is an education in the faith for both children and adults that teaches Christian doctrine through a series of questions and answers. For use with children today, the simplest form is the *Small Children's Catechism*. Also, there are the *Catechism for Young Children* and the *Shorter Catechism*. All versions are available online at http://www.reformed.org/documents/index.html.

4. Routinely discuss with your child how to reason with truth and apply Christian doctrine to the questions and choices they face every day. With older children and youth, discuss the implications of a biblical worldview for family issues like marriage and sexuality and cultural issues like government, economics, art, music, science, etc. A helpful resource is *Training Hearts, Teaching Minds*. Other worldview-training materials are available from the Nehemiah Institute: http://www.nehemiahinstitute.com and Summit Ministries http://www.summit.org.

5. Parents' worldview has the greatest impact on the development of the child's worldview. Make sure that *your own thinking* is shaped by the biblical worldview! George Barna estimates that only 8 percent of Christians in the United

States have a biblical worldview! An excellent family resource for discussion between parents that can be simplified for children is Charles Colson and Nancy Pearcey's *How Now Shall We Live?*[145] The book includes a study guide of worldview questions that will provoke thought and help the family think about the world the way God does.

6. If your church or a group of parents and youth in your neighborhood want to participate in a 12–lesson, DVD-based course of worldview training, see *The Truth Project*[146] developed by Focus on the Family, now available in a number of languages.

Gate ten: Your Child's Gender Identity

Personal identity is the sum total of one's view of himself. Because we are created in the image of God with rich and diverse dimensions, no single aspect of our being should dominate our view of ourselves. While we are not primarily sexual beings, our maleness or femaleness is an integral and vital dimension of our total person.

God presents Himself as male. He revealed Himself through a son, not a daughter. We have a perfect model of maleness in the person of Jesus Christ. Yet God's nature contains both male and female characteristics.[147] *"God created man in His own image, in the image of God He created him; male and female He created them"* (Genesis 1:27). The relationship between male and female in the creation order of Genesis is reaffirmed in the New Testament by Jesus[148] and Paul.[149] God sovereignly chooses the gender of every child.[150] A child's gender is key to God's purpose and call on his life. A child's *acceptance of his gender* is equally critical. The development of healthy gender identity is rooted in the loving relationship between a child's father and the mother and in the child's own relationship with each parent. The parents' healthy relationship with one another should model mutual respect as they fulfill their God-given, complementary roles within the family. There is no difference in honor, glory, or value between male and female.[151]

One of Satan's primary strategies for perverting the image of God in children is to confuse their gender identity. The enemy has so infiltrated the culture with his deceptions about sexual orientation that even the Church has begun to accept homosexuality. When the Church abandons this gate, the whole culture becomes vulnerable. The governments of many nations uphold the lie that a person can choose his sexual orientation and gender. This propaganda is promoted as a civil right, but the truth is that only God has the authority to determine gender. The Apostle Paul describes what is happening in our nations as the result of suppressing the truth about God:

> *Therefore God gave them over in the lusts of their hearts to impurity, so that their bodies would be dishonored among them. For they exchanged the truth of God for a lie, and worshipped and served the creature rather than the Creator, who is blessed forever. Amen. For this reason God gave them over to degrading passions; for their women exchanged the natural function for that which is unnatural, and in the same way also the men abandoned the natural function of the woman and burned in their desire toward one another, men with men committing indecent acts and receiving in their own persons the due penalty of their error. And just as they did not see fit to acknowledge God any longer, God gave them over to a depraved mind, to do those things which are not proper.* (Romans 1:24–28)

The young child's sexual identity must be guarded by the loving acceptance of his parents and by true worship of the living God. The child's view of sexuality must be firmly rooted in the Word of God, and ungodly sexual norms of culture must be clearly rejected. What the child is taught in school must be carefully monitored. Once a child is established in his own gender identity and knows that God chooses each person's gender, he needs to be taught how to keep himself sexually pure and how to interact lovingly with persons who are deceived.

Guarding your child's sexual identity gate

1. If you were disappointed in your child's gender at birth, repent of this attitude, give thanks to God for the boy or girl He gave you, and delight in your child as that boy or girl!

2. If the father is absent from your home, ask the Lord to provide the loving male affirmation and blessing that

each child needs in addition to the mother's affirmation and blessing.

3. Cultivate a worshipful heart in your child, not only during family worship but by praising God's attributes in creation when you are outdoors, or when observing the wisdom and beauty of what He has made. Although man is unique as God's image bearer, creation offers many lessons in sexuality, including its purpose and fruitfulness.

4. In your family's devotional time, be sure to interact with your child about God's image, how He created us male and female and chose our gender. Study how God intends male and female to complement one another in His divine order. When your child is at an appropriate age, include a study of Romans 1.

5. Before school starts each year (whether public or Christian), get a copy of the sex education curriculum for your child's grade level. Prayerfully consider what the Lord would have you opt your child out of if you can do so in your nation. If not, follow the school's lessons with your own teaching at home and discern whether your child is able to withstand the deceptions taught at school.

6. Screen television programs, films, and internet sites carefully for illicit sexual behaviors. Otherwise, consider removing television and internet access until your child is a mature youth, well grounded in his relationship with Jesus Christ.

7. If your youth has already chosen a homosexual or transgender identity, do not give up! He can be healed and transformed by the power of Christ[152] through repentance and prayer.

Closing Thoughts

What is God saying about the various gates to your child's heart? Which gates are well guarded and nurtured in your home? Which are vulnerable? We have all failed to watch over certain areas of our child's life, but now is the time to be like Nehemiah and seek the Lord for wisdom, help, and courage to repair the gates and restore the wall. God eagerly awaits our repentance and our commitment to enter into covenant, as Nehemiah did, so that He can provide the help and guidance needed.[153] The following simple prayer may be of help:

Dear heavenly Father, I welcome Your plan to nurture my child and raise him up as a leader in his generation. I confess that I have fallen short of my role as a parent to nurture and guard the gates of his heart, and I repent. I turn now to You, asking for Your grace and power to be a parent after Your heart. Help me to cast vision for my child's life based on Your eternal call and according to Your eternal Word. Give me the wisdom and resources to establish his identity in Christ and to equip him to fulfill Your purpose for his life. May he attain His full potential in Christ. Be glorified in our family and in the next generation. Amen.

Additional Resources

AMO® Bible reading for reasoning, literature, and Christian history curricula (available in English, Spanish, and Portuguese): http://www.amoprogram.com

Youth with a Mission. *Christian Heroes: Then and Now.* Seattle, Wash.: YWAM Publishing.

Christianhomeschoolers.com. *Online Biographies of Famous People.* http://www.christianhomeschoolers.com/hs_biographies.html

Christian Classics Ethereal Library. http://www.ccel.org/index/subject/classics

Sky.fm (free classical internet radio channel). http://www.sky.fm/classical

CHAPTER 9

ESTABLISHING FAMILY WORSHIP

God established the home as a center for worship from which His blessings flow into the community and nation. He chose the Christian family to proclaim His praises and reproduce His love and righteousness in the world. When God called Abraham and his family to worship Him, He spoke this wonderful promise:

> *"And I will make you a great nation,*
> *And I will bless you,*
> *And make your name great;*
> *And so you shall be a blessing;*
> *And I will bless those who bless you . . .*
> *And in you all the families of the earth will be blessed."*
> (Genesis 12:2–3)

God has given parents the capacity to reproduce children after His heart and nature. He has given fathers responsibility to teach children His ways and has provided them with the necessary guidance for success. In the same way, He has planted in the heart of every child a yearning to know and worship Him. In every marvelous detail, God designed and prepared the family unit for worship and blessing.

In creation, God gave man the capacity
to produce children after His own likeness

God created man, male and female,[154] in His own image, each reflecting unique aspects of His own loving and relational nature. From the beginning, God blessed parents with the divine capacity to produce children after their own likeness.[155] Families on Earth are to reflect the glorious and mysterious life of the godhead in the fellowship of the Father, Son, and Holy Spirit. Adam and Eve delighted in this close fellowship before they sinned. When they disobeyed God, all of humanity inherited a sinful nature. However, God's Father-heart had already planned man's redemption and the restoration of intimate fellowship with God through Christ. Over many generations, God patiently cultivated His people's faith and understanding through a series of covenants that reveal the requirements of relationship with God and His rich blessings. Let us examine these covenant promises.

By God's covenant with fathers of faith,
the family is His instrument of blessing

"By faith Noah . . . built an ark to save his family" (Hebrews 11:7). Noah is an example of how the faith of righteous parents obtains a blessing for their children. God delivered Noah and his family from the great flood that destroyed all mankind except for the eight people in the ark. In thanksgiving, Noah built an altar and led his family in worship. God covenanted with Noah that He would not again destroy the Earth by flood. God blessed Noah and his sons and populated the whole Earth through their family!

God also made a covenant with Abraham, to give him a son through whom God's blessings would be passed to the nations.[156] God said, *"I will establish My covenant between Me and you and your descendants after you throughout their generations for an a everlasting covenant, to be God to you and to your descendants after you"* (Genesis 17:7). Note that the covenant was not only with the father, but also with his children and grandchildren. The covenant is a promise backed by God's faithfulness. God purposes to have the same relationship with the child as with the father. The promise, *"I will be your God,"* is accepted by the father's faith in God's faithfulness. The parent accepts this promise also for his child. God assures the parent of

His grace to help bring the child into the same personal faith in God. In the New Covenant that God made through the sacrifice of Jesus Christ, all who believe in Christ are also *"heirs . . . of the covenant"*[157] and recipients of every covenant blessing.

By God's appointment, fathers and husbands are priests to their families

While every Christian is a priest, husbands and fathers have a special priestly ministry as heads of their households. God has set fathers apart as priests in their homes in order to initiate His blessings in the family. The priestly ministry of the father springs from his own faith, which enables him to trust in God's covenant. The father's faith and love for God precede God's command to teach their children: *"You shall love the Lord your God with all your heart and with all your soul and with all your might"* (Deuteronomy 6:5).

As priest of the family, the father serves in three ways. First, he intercedes on behalf of the children to bring blessings on them. We have a poignant example of the father's intercessory role in the Passover, when God instructed Moses to have all the heads of households put the blood of an unblemished male lamb on the door frames of their houses. Fathers offered this blood sacrifice in faith that God would protect the family from the plagues that fell upon Egypt.[158] The Passover lamb foretells the sacrifice of Jesus Christ, the Lamb of God.[159] By faith in the power of the blood of Jesus, Christian fathers obtain God's promised blessings on behalf of their own families.

Second, fathers have a priestly role as teachers. They are appointed to give instruction in godliness to their children. The teaching role of parents is discussed more fully in previous chapters. Third, fathers have a priestly role as worship leaders of their families. The Bible's first mention of the word "worship" appears in the story of Abraham taking Isaac to Mt. Moriah.[160] God had asked Abraham to sacrifice Isaac in worship. As father and son departed Isaac asked, *"Where is the lamb for the burnt offering?"* Based on previous times of worship, Isaac knew a sacrifice was needed. Abraham told Isaac, *"God will provide for Himself the lamb"* (Genesis 22:7–8). Isaac learned to trust God through the example and teaching of his father. Both he and his son Jacob led their own families in worshipping the Lord.[161]

True worship is a way of life motivated by love and obedience

The dictionary defines the verb *worship* as "to adore; to pay divine honors to; to reverence with supreme respect and veneration."[162] We worship God when we ascribe worth to Him. Worship involves our whole being and every area of life.

> *I urge you, brethren, by the mercies of God, to present your bodies a living and holy sacrifice, acceptable to God, which is your spiritual service of worship. And do not be conformed to this world, but be transformed by the renewing of your mind, so that you may prove what the will of God is, that which is good and acceptable and perfect.* (Romans 12:1–2)

Our supreme act of worship is to obey God from a heart of love. Jesus says, *"If you love me you will keep my commandments."*[163] We may fall short, but God has provided a sacrifice for our failure and short-comings. The first fathers in the Bible sacrificed animals such as goats, calves, and lambs to atone for their sins. These were merely a shadow of the one true sacrifice, the blood of Christ: *"Christ entered the Most Holy Place only once—and for all time. He did not take with him the blood of goats and calves. His sacrifice was his own blood, and by it he set us free from sin forever"* (Hebrews 9:12 New Century Version). By faith in the blood of Jesus, our hearts are made clean. *"Therefore let us draw near with confidence to the throne of grace, so that we may receive mercy and find grace to help in time of need"* (Hebrews 4:16).

worship (v.) To adore; to reverence; to supreme-ly respect; to honor with love and devotion.

Family devotions are a key element of family worship

The parent's heart of praise, thanksgiving, and joyful dependency upon God in daily life imparts a spirit of worship to the child. In addition, a daily time of praise, teaching the Word, and prayer draws children directly into a worshipful and personal relationship with God. Devotions are led by the head of the household. If the father is absent, the mother leads. Leading family devotions is not complicated. Here are some principles and ideas to help you begin or to strengthen the family devotional time you already have.

PRINCIPLE 1:
Idols and altars to other gods must be removed

Anything we place on an equal footing with or above the Lord God is an idol. All good things—family, a successful career, a romantic relationship, beauty, and material possessions—are God's gifts; they must not take the place of God in our lives. Timothy Keller says, "An idol is whatever you look at and say in your heart of hearts, 'If I have that, then I'll feel my life has meaning, then I'll know I have value, then I'll feel significant and secure.'"[164] When we believe that other things will satisfy us more than Him, we are deceived. This deception opens us to value and pursue counterfeit gods.

> "You shall have no other gods before Me. You shall not make for yourself an idol, or any likeness of what is in heaven above or on the earth beneath or in the water under the earth. You shall not worship them or serve them; for I, the Lord your God, am a jealous God, visiting the iniquity of the fathers on the children, and on the third and the fourth generations of those who hate Me." (Deuteronomy 5:7-9)

We were created with the built-in desire to worship God. Either we worship God, or we create our own gods to worship. While the idolatrous worship of graven images is blatantly evil,[165] the Bible also identifies other sins as idolatry: "immorality, impurity, passion, evil desire, and greed" (Colossians 3:5). We make money an idol when it becomes an end in itself.[166] God's gift of sexuality attains idol status when we fail to honor our bodies or guard our minds from sexual impurity. Our bodies are "temples of the Holy Spirit" to be honored as such (1 Corinthians 6:19). Pornography and sex outside marriage are idolatry. We are guilty of idolatry when we use our abilities, position, or authority to manipulate or control others.

altar (n.) A place of worship. For the believer, the altar is one's heart.

idol (n.) Anything that usurps the place of God in the hearts of men.

Throughout history, the devil has seduced people to worship him under the guise of other gods.[167] Some homes have actual altars where images of false deities are worshipped. The Bible says that these images of wood, gold, or silver are dead; they have no breath.[168] All idolatry robs the Lord of the worship of which He alone is worthy.

Applying this principle in your life

Repentance for idolatry opens the way for worship that is pleasing to the Lord.

1. Ask the Lord to show you anything you or your family has allowed to interfere with your worship of Him.[169] Repent of these idols, asking God's forgiveness, and then act on your assurance of that forgiveness by renewing your worship of God alone.

2. Ask the Lord to sanctify your home with the Holy Spirit. Ask Him to show you what objects, images, or music should be removed and destroyed.

3. Dedicate your home in prayer to the Lord.

PRINCIPLE 2:
Praise and thanksgiving open the way into God's Presence

We approach the Lord in family worship with joy and boldness because we have been cleansed of our sins. We have been made holy by the sacrificial blood of Jesus Christ! Thanksgiving and praise are the sacrifices that honor and please God.[170]

> *Enter His gates with thanksgiving*
> *And His courts with praise.*
> *Give thanks to Him, bless His name.* (Psalm 100:4)

> *O come, let us sing for joy to the Lord,*
> *Let us shout joyfully to the rock of our salvation.*
> *Let us come before His presence with thanksgiving,*
> *Let us shout joyfully to Him with psalms.* (Psalm 95:1–2)

The New Testament likewise exhorts us to sing psalms, hymns, and spiritual songs to God.[171] We worship the Lord with songs of praise and adoration, with words extolling God's character and magnifying His mighty deeds, with musical instruments, and with dance. The Lord lives in the praises of His people.[172] The Holy Spirit draws near as a Christian family praises the Lord.[173]

Applying this principle in your life

Consider these ideas for cultivating a spirit of praise and thanksgiving in family worship:

1. Call the family to worship by reading a verse of praise, expressing your need and longing for God, and inviting the Lord's Presence. (See resources in the sample devotion at the end of this chapter.)

2. Speaking or singing scriptural songs to the Lord is a wonderful way to worship Him. The psalms are full of praise. Hymnals or songbooks are useful. Many praise and worship songs are in the public domain and can be found on the internet. Once children have learned the first stanza and refrain, a new one can be introduced, but be sure to sing the ones they have already learned and build a repertoire. (See resources in the sample family devotion at the end of this chapter.)

3. Encourage your children to tell God in their own words what they are thankful for. Model this kind of praise.

4. The Holy Spirit may give a member of the family a new song, a Scripture of praise to share, or spontaneous words of love for God.[174] Children may write a song or poem of praise to the Lord or play an instrument in worship.

5. At first, parents will want to select praise songs or hymns and lead the worship. Once the pattern is established, older children may share in the role of leading praise and thanksgiving.

PRINCIPLE 3:
Opening the Word together builds a strong family

God wants each of your children to develop a personal relationship with Him based on the gospel.[175] If our families are to be strong, His commandments must be taught and obeyed. God ordained that parents be their children's primary teachers of the Word.

> *"Now this is the commandment, the statutes and the judgments which the Lord your God has commanded me to teach you, that you might do them in the land where you are going over to possess it, so that you and your son and your grandson might fear the Lord your God, to keep all His statutes and His commandments which I command you, all the days of your life, and that your days may be prolonged. O Israel, you should listen and be careful to do it, that it may be well with you and that you may multiply greatly, just as the Lord, the God of your fathers, has promised you, in a land flowing with milk and honey."* (Deuteronomy 6:1–3)

As parents look to the Bible themselves for instruction and search in it for wisdom, we model for our children the truth of Psalm 119:105, *"Your word is a lamp to my feet and a light to my path."* Christian parents cherish and teach God's Word above the thoughts and opinions of man.[176] Christians who did not grow up reading the Bible may never have learned to think and reason with biblical principles. However, we can learn to think like God by daily reading and meditating on His Word and obeying all that we understand. Over time our minds are renewed by the Word of God.[177] Often we limit our thinking by viewing the Bible as merely personal and private rather than seeing its great relevance to every area of life. God cares about all of life, including our work, marriage, friendships, health, finances, and the government of our cities and nations. He has wisdom and guidance for every decision, choice, and problem. As we study His Word, meditate upon it, and pray, God will give vision and wisdom to our family and make us a blessing of light and salt to others.

Applying this principle in your life

Here are some suggestions to consider in opening the Word of God to your family.

1. Varied daily Scripture reading plans are available. (See resources in sample devotion at the end of this chapter.) A simple approach is to read a portion of a chapter a day, choosing the key paragraphs. Alternate between Old and New Testament Scriptures, and omit those that are not suitable for family worship, e.g., long genealogies.

2. Read a portion of Scripture and explain the words or concepts your children do not understand. Younger children find Bible stories particularly meaningful, yet almost any short passage can hold their attention if read with enthusiasm and interpretation.

3. Follow the Bible reading with simple questions that help your children reflect on truth and apply it to their own circumstances. Provoke them to interact with the Word!

4. Choose a verse to memorize as a family, and devote time during family worship for one or more children to recite it. Many Scripture rhymes and songs provide fun ways to memorize the Word. (For Scripture memory resources, see this resource: https://www.thelearningparent.com/products.asp?cat = 43.)

5. Provide your children with a binder to file key memory verses, favorite hymns and songs, and what the Lord has spoken to them during family worship. This will be a treasure for leading their own children in family worship someday.

6. Recite together one of the historic Christian creeds, one of the Ten Commandments, or one of the questions and answers from the Westminster Shorter Catechism. (See resources in the sample devotion at the end of this chapter.)

PRINCIPLE 4:
Praying with your children builds relationship with God

Our Lord is a God of relationship, and He has given us prayer as a means for knowing Him intimately. He longs for us to talk to Him as our heavenly Father, and He delights in answering when we call upon Him. The word "prayer" is first mentioned in Scripture in King David's response to God's promise to bless his family line: "For You, O Lord of hosts, the God of Israel, have made a revelation to Your servant, saying, 'I will build you a house'; therefore Your servant has found courage to pray this prayer to You" (2 Samuel 7:27). Our supreme example of fellowship in prayer is that which Jesus daily had with the Father.[178] When His disciples asked Him to teach them to pray, He replied:

> "Pray, then, in this way: 'Our Father who is in heaven, Hallowed be Your name. Your kingdom come. Your will be done, on earth as it is in heaven. Give us this day our daily bread. And forgive us our debts, as we also have forgiven our debtors. And do not lead us into temptation, but deliver us from evil. [For Yours is the kingdom and the power and the glory forever. Amen]." (Matthew 6:9–13)

As Jesus taught His disciples, we model for our children the elements of prayer: praise, thanksgiving, confession, asking forgiveness, and petition for our needs. Our words in prayer come simply and sincerely from our hearts. Prayer opens the way for children to grow in a personal relationship with God. They need to know that He is always available, that He is holy and hates sin, but that He always loves them deeply and is ready to forgive. Children need to know that God wants them to cast all their cares on Him. They need to know that they can ask Him for help in anything and He will be faithful. Children need the opportunity to confess their sins and ask God's forgiveness. As they experience God's answers to their prayers, they grow in trust and faith.

An atmosphere of loving support enhances family prayer time. As family members forgive one another, they learn the power of forgiveness to heal strained relationships. Family prayer is a time to ask the Lord to establish the Word in your child's daily thinking and habits. It is also a time for parents to pray *with* children, blessing them, asking for God's protection over them, and for God's wisdom in their daily lives and choices. Parents know the particular needs of each child and what type of encouragement and direction will build them up. Your children need to hear *you* pray for them. A father and mother's prayers *with* their children build strong family bonds in Christ.

Applying this principle in your life

Consider these ideas for family worship to cultivate in your child a relationship with God through prayer:

1. Incorporate the scriptural passage that was read and discussed during family worship in prayer.

2. Read aloud from the Scriptures about the benefits of confession of sin and forgiving others.[179]

3. Use scriptural expressions of confession, pleas for forgiveness and pardon, and petitions.

4. Pray scriptural prayers over your children. Show your children how to keep a prayer journal to record God's direction for guidance.

5. Provide time for your children to pray for family needs and for others.

6. Invite your children to share God's answers to their prayers.

A Sample Family Devotion

Family devotions are not a ritual with an unchangeable form. Allow the Holy Spirit to guide your family worship time. For those who desire an order with which to begin, consider the sample below from *The Family Worship Book* by Terry Johnson. The entire worship need not last more than 15 to 20 minutes. A short period each day is more effective than one hour every two weeks.

1. Call to worship and a prayer praising the attributes of God

    Scriptures of Praise
    Psalm 145:18; Isaiah 57:15a; Habakkuk 2:20; Malachi 1:11; John 4:24; Romans 12:1; Hebrews 12:28; Psalm 8:1; Psalm 19:1; Psalm 24:1-2; Psalm 90:1; Psalm 95:6-7a; Psalm 124:8; Revelation 4:11; Exodus 34:6b-7; 1 Chronicles 29:11-13; James 1:17; Revelation 4:8b; Ephesians 1:3-6; Colossians 1:13-20; Revelation 5:9, 10, 12, 13b; Psalm 18:1-3; Psalm 27:4, 8; Psalm 42:1-2a; Psalm 46:1; Psalm 63:1-4; Psalm 84:1-4, 10-12

2. Singing of hymns/worship and praise songs

    Historic Hymns
    The lyrics, audio melodies, and piano scores can be found by searching titles at http://www.hymnsite.com/lyrics/:

"A Mighty Fortress Is Our God"
"Alas! and Did My Savior Bleed"
"All Hail the Power of Jesus' Name"
"Amazing Grace"
"Christ the Lord Is Risen Today"
"Crown Him with Many Crowns"
"Great Is Thy Faithfulness"
"Holy, Holy, Holy!"
"O for a Thousand Tongues to Sing"

3. Confession of a creed or commandment

The Apostles' Creed
The Nicene Creed
The Westminster Shorter Catechism
(Others available online at www.reformed.org/documents)
The Ten Commandments: Exodus 20:2–17;
    Deuteronomy 5:6–21
The Beatitudes (Jesus' teaching): Matthew 5:1–10

4. Scripture reading and reflection questions

http://www.wholesomewords.org/family/bibleread/
    truth.html
https://www.YouVersion.com (Bible reading plans applica-
    tion for mobile devices)

5. Prayers of thanksgiving, confession, and intercession

Confession and Forgiveness
Exodus 34:9; Numbers 14:19; Numbers 32:23; Psalm 19:12–
13; Psalm 38:3b–4; Psalm 51:1–17; Psalm 69:5; Psalm 79:9;
Psalm 130:3–4a; Psalm 139:23–24; Daniel 9:5, 8–11a, 17–19;
Ezra 9:6; Nehemiah 9:33–34; Luke 15:21; Luke 18:13

Promises of Pardon
Psalm 32:1–2, 5; Psalm 103:8, 10–12; Isaiah 38:17b; Isaiah
43:25; Isaiah 53:5, 6; Romans 5:1; Romans 8:1; Titus 3:5–7;
1 Peter 2:24; 1 John 1:8–9; 1 John 2:1–2

Petitions
Government and community leaders (1 Timothy 2:1–2)
Christian ministry (Matthew 9:36–38)
Salvation (1 Timothy 2:1–4)

Sanctification (Ephesians 6:18; Philippians 1:9–11;
Colossians 1:9–11; Ephesians 1:15–23)
Healing (James 5:13–18; 2 Corinthians 1:3–11)

6. Benediction or a blessing

"Doxology" lyrics, audio melody, and piano score:
http://www.hymnsite.com/lyrics/umh095.sht
"Gloria Patri" lyrics, audio melody, and piano score:
http://www.hymnsite.com/lyrics/umh070.sht
Aaronic Blessing: Numbers 6:24–26
Apostolic Blessing: 2 Corinthians 13:14

Closing Thoughts

What is God showing you about your family's worship? He is eager to
reveal Himself to our children and family and to capture our hearts as
we adoringly gaze upon Him and humble ourselves to learn from Him.
If you have a desire to initiate a time of family devotions or to enrich
what you are already doing, you may want to pray something like this:

*Dear Lord, You alone are worthy of worship! Thank You for com-
missioning me as a parent with the privilege of being a priest to
my family. Forgive me where I have fallen short. I desire to teach
my children Your ways in the Bible and to instruct them how to
pray. I dedicate myself afresh in this important arena of family life.
Please guide and inspire me in ways that will draw my children to
love You and desire to worship You their whole lives. Amen.*

Additional Resources

Alexander, James W. *Thoughts of Family Worship.* Morgan, Pa: Soli Deo Gloria
Publications, 1998.

Baucham, Voddie T. Jr. *Family Driven Faith: Doing What It Takes to Raise Sons
and Daughters Who Walk with God.* Wheaton, Ill: Crossway Books, 2007.

Beeke, Joel R. *Family Worship.* Grand Rapids, Mich.: Reformation Heritage
Books, 2002.

Brown, Scott. *Family Reformation.* Wake Forest, North Carolina: Merchant
Adventurers, 2009.

Henry, Matt. *A Church in the House: Restoring Daily Worship to the Christian Household.* San Antonio, Tex.: The Vision Forum, 2007. (Also available online at http://andrewgroves.files.wordpress.com/2008/09/a-church-in-the-house-_-mathew-henry.pdf)

Johnson, Terry L. *The Family Worship Book.* Geanies House, Great Britain: Christian Focus Publications, 1998.

Koelman, Jacobus. *The Duties of Parents.* Grand Rapids, Mich.: Reformation Heritage Books, 2003.

Moore, E. Ray, and Gail Pinckney Moore. *The Promise of Jonadab.* Greenville, Sc: Ambassador International, 2010.

Murray, Andrew. *How to Bring Your Child to Christ.* Springdale, Ark.: Whitaker House, 1984.

CHAPTER 10

CELEBRATING FAMILY TRADITIONS AND GODLY HERITAGE

The home is the womb in which every child's knowledge of God, others, and self is formed. The Christian home is where God's providence should first be introduced and celebrated. In the context of family relationships and traditions, strong bonds are established that affect the inner health of the child's soul and give him a sense of purpose and belonging. Initiating and celebrating family traditions establishes the child's faith within his family heritage. Family traditions are customs, beliefs, practices, and stories that are handed down from one generation to another. Most often, they are linked to special events such as birthdays, anniversaries, and national and religious holidays. However, they can be as simple as sitting down for dinner together and staying connected through pleasant conversation. When celebrated over the years, these traditions evoke strong emotions and bind us together as a family unit throughout our lives. The fast-paced, busy lifestyle in which many of us live has crowded out the time needed to plan and prepare meals and activities for quality family time. Perhaps this is one of the contributing factors to the breakdown of families in our nations.

God is a God of remembrance and celebration. We know this from studying His Word. He delights in festivals and feasts, having instituted seven feasts in Israel that foreshadowed the coming of His Messiah and foretold of His plan of salvation and redemption. He ordained these biblical feasts to be a "perpetual statute" and to be celebrated throughout all generations (Leviticus 23:14). Sharing God's testimonies with our children and celebrating the birth, death, and resurrection of Jesus Christ each year are essential to our spiritual growth and health. In the Old Testament, after Nehemiah rebuilt the walls of Jerusalem and the high priest, Ezra, read God's Law to all the Israelite families, Nehemiah called for a celebration to memorialize the providence and mercy of the living God toward His people.

tradition (n.) The delivery of beliefs, stories, practices, and customs from father to son, or from ancestors to posterity.

> *Then he said to them, "Go, eat of the fat, drink of the sweet, and send portions to him who has nothing prepared; for this day is holy to the Lord. Do not be grieved, for the joy of the Lord is your strength."... And all the people went away to eat, to drink, to send portions and to celebrate a great festival, because they understood the words which had been made known to them.* (Nehemiah 8:10, 12)

The testimony of God's mighty works in the birth of Israel as a nation was recorded for the benefit of every generation that followed. In fact, God gave instructions to fathers to tell of His wondrous works to their children and grandchildren, lest His people forget His miracles and mighty Hand in their lives and in their history as His people. When we forget His Hand in our lives and in the history of our nations, we become an ungrateful and unhealthy people.

celebrate (v.) To praise; to extol; to commend; to honor with ceremonies of joy and respect.

> *I will open my mouth in a parable; I will utter dark sayings of old, which we have heard and known, and our fathers have told us. We will not conceal them from their children, but tell to the generation to come the praises of the Lord, and His strength and His wondrous works that He has done.* (Psalm 78:2–4)

In the New Testament, Jesus' disciples celebrated His resurrection at the conclusion of their weekly *agape* meal by breaking bread and drinking from the' cup of wine, as He had shared with them at His Last Supper (Matthew 26:26–29; 1 Corinthians 11:24, 25). This practice is a way of remembering Christ's sacrifice and of celebrating His life, death, and resurrection.

We remember God's hand in our own families, and take joy in their lives. Every family has a story that needs to be told. God is the Master Storyteller, the Author of "His story," and He placed within man a love of story. Special events, birthdays, and holiday celebrations provide us many opportunities to share our story and keep alive the history that makes each family unique and each family member special. This is one way to establish meaningful and loving family traditions. It is part of a child's sense of wellbeing and wholeness to memorialize and celebrate his family's heritage and to learn the stories behind family heirlooms. Heirlooms are objects that provide a personal attachment to a family member that is loved and revered, usually someone who is no longer living. They are often passed from generation to generation. The symbolic and repetitive aspects of family heirlooms, customs, and traditions engrave values, ethnic character, and the significance of historical events on the heart of the child.

heritage (n.) That valued portion, share, and way of life inherited from one's forefathers.

Children have keen memories, and they love reflecting upon the activities and meals that they experience at feasts, festivals, and family celebrations. These traditions provide wonderful memories of joyful family fellowship that strengthen both family bonds and the child's identification with the eternal family of God. Partaking in family traditions and celebrations also trains the child to reach beyond his own family to serve others in the neighborhood and the larger community.

PRINCIPLE 1:
Endearing family traditions must be intentionally cultivated in the home by parents and grandparents

Family traditions worth remembering and passing down to the next generation must be intentionally planned and carried out. They do not just happen by themselves. Ancient Jewish families believed that *"children are an heritage of the Lord"* (Psalm 127:3 KJV) and therefore invested much love and instruction of their revered traditions at every stage of development. They set in motion family traditions that are still practiced today by many Jews. At the birth of a child, parents chose a birth Scripture that they taught to the child at a very young age. Toddlers followed their mothers around during the week and at festival times learned the songs and traditions of the feast days. The weekly Sabbath meal, the lighting of the Sabbath lamp, the reading of Scripture, and the setting apart of a portion of the dough from the bread for the household are simple examples of what the young Jewish child learned at home as his heritage and family traditions. We learn of the tremendous influence of family traditions through the lives of Moses and Daniel, who both were educated in pagan courts as boys but held strong to their early childhood influences and traditions as national leaders in a pagan environment. This was the fruit of the faithful and intentional investment of their parents and grandparents, who took seriously their role to pass their godly heritage and family traditions down to their children and grandchildren.

Daily home life is the most vital source of family tradition for nourishing the child's identity and strengthening family bonds. God is honored in the home as families cherish mealtime together, family devotions, games and activities, hosting others in the home, and family travel. The everyday sharing of familial love in Christ is the bedrock of a child's life. The traditions that parents establish for their own children are passed on when their grown children become tradition-setters in their own homes.

Applying this principle in your life

Consider these ideas for enriching the traditions of your own home life:

1. Sit with your spouse and create a yearly plan for cultivating and celebrating your family heritage and the life of each of your individual family members.

2. Plan at least one meal a day together to enjoy one another's fellowship and to pray for one another. Make the conversation pleasant and stimulating. Bring up topics that are engaging and nurturing for children.

3. Maintain a family prayer journal with the dates of prayer requests, as well as the dates they were answered.

4. Read the great children's classics aloud to your children after dinner or before bedtime. This is an activity that everyone, young and old, enjoys and by which all are nurtured.

5. Plan a birthday party that celebrates the individuality of the family member being honored. There are hundreds of ways to appreciate and honor our loved ones that don't cost money, such as creating a timeline, enacting a drama about their lives, writing a short story or poem about them, cooking a favorite meal or dessert, or doing something with the family that he loves to do. Always pray for the individual and have each one speak a blessing to him for the next year.

6. Pets give opportunity for each member of the family to learn responsibility to care in some way for another. They also bring joy and humorous memories to the family.

7. Vacations are an opportunity to celebrate God's creation together as a family and to learn the geography, culture, and history of a new area. Have your child journal his vacation experience, or if he is not yet literate, you write the journal as he dictates the highlights of each day. Give him a sketchbook to keep visual memories of his travels.

8. Music, crafts, and art enrich the home. Teach your child the skills you have acquired yourself (playing a musical instrument, sewing, woodworking, painting, etc.). Hang a copy of a famous painting each month and celebrate the artist and his style. Have evenings of poetry reading and ask each family member to read a favorite poem and elaborate on why they chose it. Have music nights where the family gathers around the piano to sing, or in some way enjoys the talents and skills that each one is developing. If your child wants to learn an instrument or craft

that you do not know, find a friend or extended family member to swap teaching: you teach the other parent's child what you know and the other parent teaches your child what he knows. Get together with the other family for a joint recital or showing of what the children are learning.

PRINCIPLE 2:
The celebration of the child's family heritage enriches his self-worth and understanding of how God has blessed his family line and prepared him for his own lifework

The child is enriched by the traditions that have been established by his parents, grandparents, and earlier forebears. Children love to hear the stories of their parents' and grandparents' lives, as well as those of other ancestors. *"Remember the days of old, consider the years of all generations. Ask your father, and he will inform you, your elders, and they will tell you"* (Deuteronomy 32:7). The generational transmission of faith and wisdom is passed on through storytelling and family traditions, remembering God's relationship with the family line. *"All the ends of the earth will remember and turn to the Lord, and all the families of the nations will worship before You"* (Psalm 22:27).

Applying this principle in your life

1. Suggest that your children interview their grandparents about specific questions, like their favorite childhood story, what they liked most to do with their family growing up, etc. Video record the interview. Take photographs. Sketch portraits of grandparents and their homestead. Write down favorite songs, recipes, and hobbies. Write a story or poem about them after the interview and make a book of remembrance. Reenact a drama about their lives for the family.

2. Make a family tree or generational timeline of ancestors and events over at least four generations. Research the cities and countries where family members were born and grew up. Note contributions your family members

made to the community or nation. Plan a family vacation to visit specific sites.

3. Show your children photos of yourself as a child, your family, and your ancestors. Make a scrapbook together of photos and information about the family's ancestors.

PRINCIPLE 3:
Christian holidays specific to your nation extend the child's celebration of God's providence beyond his own family line to the Christian heritage in his culture

Children and youth of the twenty-first century are sorely lacking in knowledge of their nations' history, especially in relation to God's mighty acts. Yet each nation has a unique providential history, the story of how Jesus Christ has been revealed in the nation, in its preservation, and in specific historic events. Many nations have established traditions rooted in Christian history that are celebrated once a year or during special seasons. These days provide special opportunities for children to see that their families and they themselves are part of God's unfolding story.

Applying this principle in your life

Here are some ideas of how to celebrate such times:

1. *National holidays of Christian heritage* (using the example of Thanksgiving in the United States): Children no longer learn the true history of Thanksgiving in school, so Thanksgiving Day provides a wonderful opportunity for the family to read or dramatize the Pilgrim story. Invite singles without a family to your home for the celebration. At mealtime, each person can write on a little strip of paper that for which they are most thankful and then have individuals draw and read each other's praises. If you decide to write anonymously, it's fun to guess whose thanksgiving is being read.

2. *Christmas*: Read or dramatize the Christmas story. Consider inviting a single parent and family to join you for

Christmas. Ask God what gift you can give to a family in your community that needs encouragement and help.

3. *New Year's Eve and Day*: How does your family bring in the New Year? Ask God in family prayer to show you His priorities for your family in the coming year. Ask Him for a Scripture-for-the-year, one that can be memorized. Periodically talk about how God is fulfilling His Word and thank Him for what He is doing. The New Year is also a good time to ask God who in the neighborhood to minister to in the coming year.

4. *Take Christian history tours* of local, state or provincial, or national sites, memorials, battlefields, etc. Stop and pray for leaders in those regions and take time to record what has been learned.

Closing Thoughts

What ideas has God stirred in your heart for enriching traditions and celebrating the heritage of your family? God knows the immense challenge to parents in the twenty-first century to maintain closeness and bonds of love. He sees the strong pressures pulling parents and children in many directions, and He wants to strengthen and bless us from within. God is jealous for us to be rooted in His family, and He delights in us when we seek to identify with Him. He has provided festival and celebration to strengthen the heart and faith of our family with joy and meaningful memories. It will take resolve and commitment to establish new traditions. If you desire to do so, simply ask the Lord for inspiration and ideas:

> *Dear Father, I desire to establish family traditions that will bind our family together in Christ and preserve the joy, richness, and wisdom of our biblical and generational heritage. I ask that You would give our family Your plan and show us where to begin. I pray that You will prepare the heart of my child to enjoy and be enriched by the things we do together each day, as well as on special occasions. Be present with us as we remember and celebrate our heritage in Jesus Christ and in our family. Amen.*

Additional Resources

Rosen, Ceil, and Moishe Rosen, *Christ in the Passover.* Chicago, Ill: Moody Bible Institute, 1978.

Samson, Robin, and Linda Pierce. *A Family Guide to Biblical Holidays.* Shelbyville, Tenn: Heart of Wisdom Publishing, 2001.

Wilson, Marvin R. *Our Father Abraham: Jewish Roots of the Christian Faith.* Grand Rapids, Mich.: Eerdmans, 1989.

CHAPTER 11

LOVING AND
SERVING OTHERS

The ultimate value in our fallen world is self-service. If fallen man's chief ambition is to be served and to use others for personal gratification, is it any wonder so many marriages are broken and families torn apart? A marriage built on a foundation of self-seeking and self-serving is unstable indeed. Completely opposite of the fallen ways of this world, the ultimate principle in God's kingdom is the loving service *of others*. God Himself sets the example. When He revealed His name to Moses on Mount Sinai, the first word with which He described Himself was "compassionate" (Exodus 34:6). *Compassion* is a compound word that literally means to suffer (*passion*) together with (*com*) another.

We see this willingness to serve, even at great cost, most clearly at the cross. God willingly gives His Son to serve and to save the lost. Christ *"made Himself nothing, taking the very nature of a servant, being made in human likeness. And being found in appearance as a man, He humbled himself and became obedient to death—even death on a cross"* (Philippians 2:7–8). Jesus said of Himself, *"Even the Son of Man did not come to be served, but to serve, and to give His life as*

love (n.) An affection of the mind excited by beauty and worth of any kind. Between certain natural relatives, love seems to be in some cases instinctive. Such is the love of a mother for her child, which manifests itself toward an infant before any particular qualities in the child are unfolded.

community (n.) A society of people having common rights and privileges, or common interests, civil, political or ecclesiastical; living under the same laws and regulations.

a ransom for many" (Mark 10:45). As followers of Christ, we have freely benefited from Christ's costly service, and we are called to imitate Him in our relationships with others. Not surprisingly, this is the secret to a happy marriage and a strong family. When each member prioritizes the needs of others and serves them in love, the result is a strong and joyful marriage and family.

God created the family to be a community of others-oriented service. Family members are to serve one another and the Body of Christ. God-fearing homes are to function as embassies of God's kingdom in the midst of a fallen world. Christian families are to reach out beyond themselves, practicing hospitality to those in need—those whom Jesus described as "the least of these" in Matthew 25. The Christian home is meant to be a place of refuge and a house of peace—a center of loving service to others.

PRINCIPLE 1:
The love of Christ compels us to love and serve others

The power of God's love is revealed throughout the Bible, most clearly in the cross of Jesus Christ:

God demonstrates His love for us in this: While we were still sinners, Christ died for us. (Romans 5:8)

As for you, you were dead in your transgressions and sins. . . . But because of His great love for us, God, who is rich in mercy, made us alive with Christ even when we were dead in transgressions—it is by grace you have been saved. (Ephesians 2:1–5)

For God so loved the world that He gave His one and only Son, that whoever believes in Him shall not perish, but have eternal life. (John 3:16)

We do not earn God's favor through our good deeds—the Bible is absolutely clear on this point. *"For by grace you have been saved through faith; and that not of yourselves, it is the gift of God; not as a result of works, so that no one may boast"* (Ephesians 2:8–9). Instead, our salvation is entirely the work of God on our behalf. While we were still opposed to God and dead in our sinfulness, He took the initiative to reconcile Himself to us. Jesus lived the perfect life we were incapable of—and His righteousness was credited to us. He died to pay the penalty that we deserved because of our sins. As a result, we are God's beloved children and members of His family entirely by grace, through faith in Christ. Our response is to simply accept Christ's love as a free and entirely underserved gift.

It is because God loves us so extravagantly and completely accepts us through Christ that we are compelled to love and serve others. In fact, our life is to be an overflow of God's love to others. We no longer use others to meet our need for significance or to fill our emptiness. All these needs and more are met by the immeasurable love of Christ for us. As we lay hold of this amazing reality, we are free to love others, not for what we will get in return but simply out of gratitude for what God has done for us. Then we are able to *"love one another as I have loved you"* (John 13:34), for *"this is how we know what love is: Jesus Christ laid down His life for us. And we ought to lay down our lives for our brothers"* (1 John 3:16). We are able to follow the example of Jesus who, though He is King of kings and Lord of lords, *"did not come to be served, but to serve, and to give His life as a ransom for many"* (Mark 10:45). This radical, sacrificial, others-serving love is possible for those who have received God's unconditional love, whose identity and purpose are deeply rooted in their relationship to Christ. Linwood Methodist Church of Kansas City, Missouri provides a specific list of what this "one another" love should look like in practice. See Appendix III.

The secret to a happy marriage and a strong family, then, is found in the gospel—in God's extravagant, unconditional, and sacrificial love toward us. His love frees us from self-centeredness to serve the needs of others, starting with those nearest to us—our spouse and our children.

Applying this principle in your life

1. Set aside a time to talk and pray with your spouse about your family's love walk with one another.

2. Ask the Lord as a family to cultivate in your hearts the love of Christ for others. If you have never received salvation through Jesus Christ, will you do so right now? Simply ask Him to forgive you of your sin and to shed His love abroad in your heart. Ask Him to be the Lord of your life and of your family. *"If you confess with your mouth Jesus as Lord, and believe in your heart that God raised Him from the dead, you will be saved"* (Romans 10:9).

PRINCIPLE 2:
God designed the family to be a community of service

God desires for our families to be nurseries that cultivate others-serving love. This begins in the relationship between husband and wife and is taught to the children by example. The husband's head-ship means that he should take the initiative in establishing a culture of service in his household, starting with how he treats his wife. In God's kingdom, headship or authority is defined by sacrificial service, not domination. Husbands are admonished to *"love your wives as Christ loved the church and gave Himself up for her"* (Ephesians 5:25). The husband is to sacrificially serve his wife, and this entails *loving* her in all the glorious depth and breadth that Christ modeled. It entails shepherding, protecting, and providing. In response, the wife is to serve her husband by willingly yielding to his leadership, showing him honor and respect, helping him carry out his vocational calling, and taking leadership in the management of the household.

Children raised in this environment learn the art of service by example—by observing how their parents prioritize the needs of one another and how they themselves are served by their parents. Parents serve their children by loving them unconditionally, by protecting them, by providing for their needs, and by educating and disciplining them. As they grow, the children serve their parents by honoring them, respecting their authority in the home, and willingly and cheerfully obeying them. Even after they have left home, children serve their parents by honoring and caring for them. Jesus' own last act before He died was to provide for His mother's future (John 19:25–27).

But how do we reconcile this with other, seemingly contradictory passages of Scripture? After all, didn't Jesus say, *"If anyone comes to*

*me and does not hate father and mother, wife and children, brothers
and sisters—yes, even their own life—such a person cannot be my disciple"* (Luke 14:26)? Didn't He say to the disciple who asked to bury
his dead father before following Him, *"Follow me and let the dead
bury their own dead"* (Matthew 8:21–22)? It would be wrong to interpret these passages as grounds to "hate" or neglect our families,
as this would be a clear violation of the oft-repeated command to
"honor your father and your mother" (Deuteronomy 5:16), as well as
of much of Jesus' own teachings on this subject (see Mark 7:6–13).
Jesus is making the important point that in the hierarchy of our devotion God comes first. In comparison to the importance of our relationship to Christ, all other relationships, including those in our families,
must pale—as important as they are. If this relational hierarchy is
disordered, things go terribly wrong. If we make our families—our
husbands, wives, or children—a "god" they will be unable to bear
the weight. As imperfect human beings, they are not able to fill the
"god shaped hole" in our hearts. God must be worshipped above all
human relationships, just as in the family the husband and wife must
prioritize their love for each other over their love for their children.

God intends this culture of loving service to extend beyond the
core relationships of husband, wife, and children. From this base,
service is to flow outward to extended family members, the Body of
Christ, neighbors, and even needy strangers. In 1 Timothy 5, Paul admonishes Christians to *"put their religion into practice by caring for
their own family and so repaying their parents and grandparents, for
this is pleasing to God"* (v. 4), and later *"If anyone does not provide
for his relatives, and especially for his immediate family, he has de-
nied the faith and is worse than an unbeliever"* (v. 8). Notice in both
passages that the scope of service extends beyond the "immediate
family" to include "relatives," with grandparents mentioned specifically. What we see from these and other passages is that God intends
the family to be the basic social safety net. God intends for the basic
needs of people to be met first within their extended families.

The story of Ruth in the Old Testament provides a beautiful illus-
tration. A severe famine has afflicted the nation of Israel, and the threat
of starvation forces Elimelech, his wife, Naomi, and their two sons off
their land. They journey to the foreign country of Moab in search of
food. During their exile, their sons marry Moabite women—of whom

one is named Ruth. Tragedy befalls Naomi when her husband dies suddenly. A short time later, both sons perish as well. She is now a widow, alone in a foreign land and utterly impoverished. In despair, she tries to persuade her daughters-in-law to start new lives with new husbands, while she returns to Israel. Out of deep loyalty and great love for her mother-in-law, Ruth chooses to remain with Naomi and travel with her to Israel.

Upon arriving, they come to land owned by Boaz, a relative of Naomi's husband and a "man of standing" (Ruth 2:1). Boaz notices Ruth in his field gleaning wheat near the end of the day. He treats Naomi and Ruth with great kindness and respect. He brings them under his protection and provides for their needs. In due time, he and Ruth marry and she bears a son. At his birth, the women of the town surround Naomi with songs of rejoicing: *"Praise be to the Lord, who this day has not left you without a kinsman-redeemer. May he become famous throughout Israel! He will renew your life and sustain you in your old age"* (Ruth 4:14–15). Ruth and Naomi are not left alone but are brought under the care, protection, and provision of Naomi's extended family in the person of Boaz.

The home-based charity portrayed in the story of Ruth is God's intention for the family. Today, this critical role has been undermined in many Western countries by government social welfare programs. While well intentioned, these programs have weakened family bonds. Instead of looking to their families for support, widows, seniors, or single parents in these nations are encouraged to look to the government, which becomes a kind of surrogate family. But impersonal and often distant government bureaucracies cannot replace the kind of local, personal, and rich support that God intends families to provide. Christian families need to reclaim their God-intended responsibilities to serve extended family members in need, rather than leaving this care to others—or to government social welfare programs.

Applying this principle in your life

Dr. Bob Moffitt, president of Harvest International, has developed a series of lessons called "The Disciplines of Love." Bob says this tool is designed to help followers of Christ practice demonstrating God's love by serving others. The image of God is best reflected in man through sacrificial servanthood. Believers should become more aware of the need to personally reflect Christ's character in four areas of God's concern (wisdom, physical, spiritual and social) in the world in which they live (family, church and community).[180]

This tool can be very helpful for guiding your family into service opportunities, whether within your extended family, in your local church, or in your community. (See additional resources at the end of this chapter.)

PRINCIPLE 3:
The family is to serve the Body of Christ and "the least of these"

God intends the family to be a community of sacrificial service, not only for its members but for the larger Body of Christ and those outside the Church as well, particularly for those whom Christ described as *"the least of these"* in Matthew 25. These include those who are impoverished and destitute (the hungry and naked), the foreigner, the sick, victims of injustice, and those in prison. In Galatians 6:10, Paul instructs all Christians: *"As we have opportunity, let us do good to all people, **especially to those who belong to the family of God"*** (emphasis added). The honorable wife of Proverbs 31 *"opens her hand to the poor and reaches out to the needy"* (v. 20). Christ-centered families are aware of needy people in their neighborhoods and communities and seek opportunities to serve them, demonstrating Christ's love in practical ways. They do this in the knowledge that the God they worship is Himself compassionate and tenderhearted toward the poor. *"A father to the fatherless, a defender of the widows, is God in His holy dwelling"* (Psalm 68:5). *"He will deliver the needy who cry out, the afflicted who have no one to help. He will take pity on the weak and the needy and save the needy from death. He will rescue them from oppression and violence, for precious is their blood in His sight"* (Psalm 72:12–14).

Local churches have a special obligation to care for the poor in their communities as well, but the first line of defense against poverty is the family. Christian families should work to ensure that the basic needs of their members are met, including extended family members. Likewise, local churches should encourage generosity among the Body of Christ and follow the example of the early Church portrayed in Acts 4:32–45. *"All the believers were one in heart and mind. No one* *claimed that any of his possessions were his own, but **they shared everything they had . . . There were no needy persons among them***" (emphasis added). In 1 Timothy 5, Paul provides very helpful training to his protégé Timothy on how the poor are to be cared for, first within the family unit and then by the Body of Christ. *"If any woman who is a believer has widows in her family, she should help them and not let the church be burdened with them, so that the church can help those widows who are really in need"* (v. 16). Who are these *"widows who are really in need"*? We can infer this to mean those who no longer have family who can care for them.

According to the Scripture, families and then local churches bear a primary responsibility to care for the poor. While government and private charity and social welfare organizations may provide additional assistance, they are not to replace the family and the local church in their responsibility to serve the poor. Such organizations tend to provide aid indiscriminately, without first-hand awareness of the needs or conditions of the poor. This tends to foster dependency, which in turn undermines the dignity of the poor and often leaves them in a worse condition. Families and local churches are in a far better position to provide real help, because they know the poor personally, and as such are able to provide aid and support in ways that distinguish between those who ought to receive help and those who might be better served with a rebuke. We see this principle, once again, in Paul's instruction to Timothy on the role of the local church:

> *Give proper recognition to those widows who are really in need. . . . No widow may be put on the list of widows* [to receive aid from the church] *unless she is over sixty, has been faithful to her husband, and is well known for her good deeds, such as bringing up her children, showing hospitality, washing the feet of the saints, helping those in trouble and devoting herself to all kinds of good deeds.* (1 Timothy 5:3, 9–10)

> *But the widow who lives for pleasure is dead even while she lives.* (1 Timothy 5:6)

Applying this principle in your life

Consider prayerfully how you can share with the poor and with those in need from the gifts and interests of your family. Involve the chil-

dren in serving guests in your home and in helping those in your
neighborhood and community. Here are some practical suggestions:

1. Practice hospitality. Regularly open your home to others
   and share a meal. Make a list of people you can invite
   that goes beyond those in your church and includes others in your neighborhood who may not know the Lord or
   who have special needs.

2. As a family, identify and commit to befriending and serving someone from the church or community with a particular need over a period of time. These might include:

   ⚬ A refugee family

   ⚬ A widow or a single mother

   ⚬ A student away from home at a college or university

   ⚬ A family or person with a serious illness

3. For larger, ongoing needs, organize with other families
   to form a "care circle" to share the load. Set up a calendar with other families to prepare meals, make visits, and
   offer other assistance.

4. Do family-based mission trips to impoverished areas of
   your community, city, or nation, or even to other nations.

5. Do a "Seed Project" as a family. Make Seed Projects a
   regular part of your family life. Integrate this activity into
   your family devotion times. (See Additional Resources at
   the end of this chapter.)

Closing Thoughts

Does loving service describe the culture of your family? How would
you like to see your family more fully involved in serving others?
What does your family enjoy doing together that could be a help or
a blessing to others? What skills do members of your family have
that could be used in serving others? Ask God for His guidance and
inspiration.

Dear Jesus, thank You for giving Your life in service to us and for teaching us that humble and loving acts of kindness are the marks of true greatness. Where our family has been overly occupied with our own needs and desires and has not considered the needs of others, forgive us. Show us how to prioritize our time as a family in ways that order our affections after Your heart. Give us Your heart of love that seeks the welfare of others so earnestly that we delight in new ways to love our neighbors as ourselves. Amen.

Additional Resources

Miller, Darrow L. *Servanthood: The Calling of Every Christian.* Available at http://www.disciplenations.org.

Moffitt, Bob, with Karla Tesch. *If Jesus Were Mayor: How Your Local Church Can Transform Your Community.* Available at http://www.disciplenations.org. See in particular Part 4: Tools for Transformation, for specific and practical tools (i.e., Disciplines of Love and Seed Projects) which you can use as a family for loving and serving others.

Zeller, Penny. *77 Ways Your Family Can Make a Difference: Ideas and Activities for Serving Others.* Kansas City, Mo.: Beacon Hill Press, 2008.

"Seed Projects." Free download available at http://www.harvestfoundation.org.

"The Disciplines of Love." Free download available at http://www.harvestfoundation.org

A Note to Single Parents and to the Church

Single parenting results from the loss of a spouse through death, military service, divorce, desertion, or imprisonment. If a woman becomes pregnant outside the covenant of marriage, she can make the courageous choice to assume the responsibility of parenting alone. If you are a single parent, you may have asked yourself if God's promises to help raise godly children are as fully available to you as they are to married parents. The answer is "yes" and "Amen" (2 Corinthians 1:20).

There is no grief or sin so deep and dark that God's grace in Christ is not deeper still. The blood of Jesus Christ has complete power to redeem each broken life and family. If it is the sin of the parent that has resulted in single motherhood or single fatherhood, our merciful God is eager to hear our repentance and to bring help and comfort. He offers forgiveness for those sins through Jesus Christ to the mother or father who accepts His salvation and Lordship. On the other hand, a parent may find herself raising children alone through no fault of her own. Regardless of the circumstances that have resulted in the absence of a father or mother, God wants to encourage you with this instruction and promise: "*Therefore, humble yourselves under the mighty hand of God, that He may exalt you at the proper time, casting all your anxiety on Him, because He cares for you*" (1 Peter 5:7).

As believers in Christ, we are taught in Scripture to look to God as our Husband, Provider, and Protector: "*For your husband is your*

Maker, Whose name is the Lord of hosts; And your Redeemer is the Holy One of Israel, Who is called the God of all the earth" (Isaiah 54:5). God promises to be "*A father of the fatherless and a judge for the widows*" (Psalm 68:5). He has a special place in His heart for parents without spouses and for children without both parents. That is why He speaks so often in the Bible to reassure parents and children in broken families. Read and meditate on the following Scriptures: Exodus 22:22–24; Deuteronomy 10:18; 27:19; Psalm 10:14–18; Isaiah 1:17; Luke 7:11–17; Acts 6:1–6; and James 1:27.

Single parents experience tremendous challenges, but their faith in Christ and His Word will enable them to overcome all obstacles and to raise children who learn the principles of the kingdom and how to find victory for themselves. What the enemy intended as destruction for the family, God can turn around and use to build a family of exceptional faith and character. Single parents who surrender to Christ and persevere in faith and biblical practice will rejoice to see their children serving the Lord as leaders in their own families and communities. However, God intends that their brothers and sisters carry the burden with them and rejoice with them at every step (Galatians 6:2; 1 Peter 4:13).

The Church is called the family of God. God created us as family so that we can reflect His own glory and nature. Single parents need whole families to come alongside them to help meet many practical needs, as well as to offer fellowship, share counsel, and pray. There is no shame in a single mother being so served. Nor is it an act of mere generosity. Such service is the direct application of the gospel; we are doing as the Father in Christ has done for us. You and I were dead in sin, totally alone, unable to believe, and devoid of righteousness. We were completely lost, completely separated from God, and without any means of making up the distance. But God in His gracious love reached down from heaven and literally stepped into our world. For the sake of His glory, He left His riches behind and embraced our human poverty so that He could provide for us all of the riches of heaven. This is why Jesus was able to say, "*Blessed are the poor in spirit for theirs is the kingdom of heaven*" (Matthew 5:3). If the Father did this for us in Christ, how can we do less? Church family, let us decide to make it a practice and a priority to help provide for God's precious single parents and their children.

Single mothers and fathers, we bless you and encourage you to make Habakkuk 3:19 your own confession of faith. Practice it daily, as you walk with God Your Husband in nurturing your child:

The Lord God is my strength,
And He has made my feet like hinds' feet,
And makes me walk on my high places.

A Word for Pastors
and Local Church Leaders

As a pastor, elder, or other church leader, your principal mission is to disciple your nation and to participate in discipling all nations. As this book makes clear, this mission is impossible without strong marriages and families. Thus our title: *As the Family Goes, So Goes the Nation.*

A clear implication, then, is that building strong marriages and families must be a priority for church leaders. God gave pastors and teachers to the church to "equip God's people for works of service, so that the body of Christ may be built up . . . " (Eph 4:12). This equipping is desperately needed in the area of marriage and family. We live in a time when this most basic, God-ordained institution is on the verge of collapse in many of our nations. How should you respond? Here are a few suggestions:

Repent. In part, marriages and families in our nations are in terrible straits because church leaders have failed to disciple their flocks in this foundational area. Rather than discipling the nations based on God's Word, churches have often been "discipled" by the prevailing trends and unbiblical, cultural norms of their nations. It is appropriate to feel sorrow and regret for this failure and to repent and ask for God's forgiveness and mercy.

Impart the biblical vision for marriage and family! This is essential. Sound biblical teaching and living examples of healthy, biblical marriages and families are both increasingly rare. The cultural messages bombarding Christians on these topics are almost entirely unbiblical. Unless pastors intentionally impart solid, biblical teaching on these core topics, most Christians will have no idea what the Bible teaches, let alone be inspired by the grand vision that God has for marriage and family in discipling nations.

Don't just teach, but model. People learn by example. What example are you setting with your marriage? Your family? Be sure you are actively working to apply and model these principles as you teach others.

Focus on husbands and fathers. God has given men inescapable leadership responsibilities in the family. Men need to be trained and equipped to carry out this role biblically and effectively. This discipleship needs to be foundational, intentional, and ongoing. Every husband and father must be reached. This training needs to extend to future husbands and fathers as well. Youth need to be trained. If pre-marital counseling doesn't impart the core biblical teaching on marriage and family in a comprehensive, winsome way, it must be changed.

Honor the leadership role of parents. Today, because of the breakdown of the family, many fathers and mothers are failing to fulfill their leadership responsibilities. Many don't know or believe that it is their primary responsibility to disciple their children. Churches (often with the best of intentions) frequently make the problem worse by saying to parents, "Don't worry, we'll disciple your children for you," and design their Sunday school and youth programs accordingly. There is certainly a place for Sunday schools and youth ministries, but it is not to carry out the job that fathers and mothers should be doing at home. Instead, focus on discipling and equipping fathers to carry out their biblical mandates. The same is true for wives and mothers.

Check your programs. Many churches segregate the family with children, youth, men, and women all receiving different teaching in different contexts. If your programs separate families, consider changing them so families can learn and grow together. It is important for families to both worship and learn together on Sunday morning.

Speak out! Join other churches and Christian organizations to defend and protect Christ-honoring marriage and family life within the broader culture. Actively support efforts that combat divorce, cohabitation, same-sex marriage, marital violence, pornography, abortion, and other destructive trends. Be a voice for biblical truth on topics of marriage, family, sexuality, and children. People are hungry to hear the truth. They are looking for hope in the midst of the wastelands of divorce and premarital sex. The church has the answer. Don't hide it. Proclaim it, not just to the congregation but to your nation as a whole.

"God's One Anothers"
from the New Testament

"If you love Me, you will obey what I command." (John 14:15)

Following is a list of thirty commands from the New Testament that overview Christ-like character and how to relate Christianly to others. When practiced, "God's One Anothers"[181] inspire successful interpersonal relationships.

"One Another"	New Testament Reference
1. Love one another	*"A new commandment I give to you, that you love one another; even as I have loved you, that you also love one another. By this all men will know that you are My disciples, if you have love for one another."* (John 13:34, 35)
2. Depend on one another	*So we, numerous as we are, are one body in Christ, the Messiah, and individually we are parts of one another—actually dependent on one another.* (Romans 12:5 AMP)
3. Be devoted to one another	*Be devoted to one another in brotherly love.* (Romans 12:10)
4. Rejoice with one another	*Rejoice with those who rejoice.* (Romans 12:15)

"One Another"	New Testament Reference
5. Weep with one another	*Weep with those who weep.* (Romans 12:15)
6. Be of the same mind toward one another	*Be of the same mind toward one another; do not be haughty in mind, but associate with the lowly. Do not be wise in your own estimation.* (Romans 12:16)
7. Give preference to one another	*Give preference to one another in honor.* (Romans 12:10)
8. Don't judge one another	*Therefore, let us not judge one another anymore, but rather determine this—not to put an obstacle or a stumbling block in a brother's way.* (Romans 14:13)
9. Accept one another	*Therefore, accept one another, just as Christ also accepted us to the glory of God.* (Romans 15:7)
10. Admonish one another	*And concerning you, my brethren, I myself also am convinced that you yourselves are full of goodness, filled with all knowledge and able also to admonish one another.* (Romans 15:14)
11. Greet one another	*Greet one another with a holy kiss.* (Romans 16:16)
12. Wait for one another	*So then, my brethren, when you come together to eat, wait for one another.* (1 Corinthians 11:33)
13. Have the same care for one another	*God has so composed the body, giving more abundant honor to that member which lacked, so that there may be no division in the body, but that the members may have the same care for one another.* (1 Corinthians 12:24, 25)
14. Be kind to one another	*Be kind to one another.* (Ephesians 4:32a)
15. Be tenderhearted to one another	*Be . . . tenderhearted, forgiving one other, just as God in Christ also has forgiven you.* (Ephesians 4:32b)
16. Serve one another	*For you were called to freedom, brethren; only do not turn your freedom into an opportunity for the flesh, but through love serve one another.* (Galatians 5:13)
17. Forgive one another	*Put on a heart of compassion, kindness, humility, gentleness and patience; bearing with one another, and forgiving each other, whoever has a complaint against anyone; just as the Lord forgave you, so also should you.* (Colossians 3:12, 13)

"One Another"	New Testament Reference
18. Encourage one another	*Therefore encourage one another and build up one another, just as you also are doing.* (1 Thessalonians 5:11)
19. Submit to one another	*Be subject to one another in the fear of Christ.* (Ephesians 5:21)
20. Uphold (forbear) one another	*Lead a life worthy of the calling to which you have been called, with all lowliness and meekness, with patience, forbearing one another in love, eager to maintain the unity of the Spirit in the bond of peace.* (Ephesians 4:1–3)
21. Stimulate one another	*Let us consider how to stimulate one another to love and good deeds.* (Hebrews 10:24)
22. Be hospitable to one another	*Be hospitable to one another without complaint.* (1 Peter 4:9).
23. Minister gifts one to another	*As each one has received a special gift, employ it in serving one another as good stewards of the manifold grace of God.* (1 Peter 4:10)
24. Be clothed in humility toward one another	*Clothe yourselves with humility toward one another, for God is opposed to the proud, but gives grace to the humble.* (1 Peter 5:5)
25. Bear one another's burdens	*Bear one another's burdens, and thereby fulfill the law of Christ.* (Galatians 6:2)
26. Do not speak against one another	*Do not speak against one another, brethren. He who speaks against a brother or judges his brother, speaks against the law and judges the law; but if you judge the law, you are not a doer of the law but a judge of it.* (James 4:11)
27. Do not complain against one another	*Do not complain, brethren, against one another, so that you yourselves may not be judged; behold, the Judge is standing right at the door.* (James 5:9)
28. Confess your sins to one another	*Confess your sins to one another.* (James 5:16a)
29. Pray for one another	*Pray for one another so that you may be healed. The effective prayer of a righteous man can accomplish much.* (James 5:16b)
30. Fellowship with one another	*If we walk in the Light as He Himself is in the Light, we have fellowship with one another, and the blood of Jesus His Son cleanses us from all sin.* (1 John 1:7)

ABOUT THE AUTHORS

Dr. Elizabeth L. Youmans

Elizabeth has served North American Christian education as a classroom teacher, school administrator, trainer of teachers, graduate school professor, curriculum writer, and editor of *The Noah Plan®*, a K–12 published Principle Approach curriculum. With over twenty years of pioneering experience in Word-centered education at the local and national level, she now imparts the vision for educational reform internationally by laying teaching and learning solidly on the foundation of Christ and His Word through her roles as founder and president of Chrysalis International, a Christian educational institute, and as creator, writer, and editor of the AMO® Program, both a worldview training program for adults and an enriched curriculum for children in English, Spanish, Portuguese, and French. She is the mother of four grown children and grandmother of seven delightful grandchildren. She currently resides in Orlando, Florida, where she is a member of St. Paul's Presbyterian Church (PCA).

Dr. Jill C. Thrift

Jill is an early childhood educator with forty years' experience whose focus has been on the parent-child relationship and early child development within the family. She has served as a preschool teacher, kindergarten supervisor, teacher trainer, bilingual education consultant, university professor, child development researcher, associate pastor, intercessor, and advocate for public policies that protect and nurture children and families. She has lived in Spain, Mexico, and Peru and has a love for the Hispanic nations. She has served on academic faculties at the University of Texas-Austin, Early Childhood Education; the University of Houston, Department of Human Development and Family Studies; the University of Texas-San Antonio, Early Childhood Education; and the University of Texas Health Science Center-San Antonio,

Pediatrics. As the single mother of a grown son, she has vision for Christian parents raising children on their own. Currently, she is an educational consultant, teacher, and writer in San Antonio, Texas.

Scott D. Allen

Scott is president of the Disciple Nations Alliance Global Secretariat. After graduating with his bachelor's degree in history from Willamette University in Salem, Oregon in 1988, Scott joined Food for the Hungry International, where he served until 2007, holding positions in both Japan and the United States in areas of human resources, staff training, and program management. Along with Darrow Miller and Bob Moffitt, Scott helped launch the Disciple Nations Alliance in 1997. He has authored and co-written a number of books, including *The Forest in the Seed: A Biblical Perspective on Resources and Development, God's Remarkable Plan for the Nations, God's Unshakable Kingdom, The Worldview of the Kingdom of God*, and *Beyond the Sacred-Secular Divide: Towards a Wholistic Life and Ministry*. Scott lives with his wife, Kim, and their five children in Phoenix, Arizona.

ACKNOWLEDGMENTS

This book would not have been possible without the wisdom, support, and encouragement of many. Special thanks go to Gary Brumbelow, our talented, humble, and hardworking editor, who spent many hours pulling together our three distinct contributions to this book with great care and skill. Gary, you kept your humor to the end and have been a special gift to us.

We would also like to thank our mutual friend, encourager extraordinaire, and "cow dog" for Christ, Rick Lane. Rick believed in the importance of this book from the beginning, helped to fund it, and kept pushing us when things bogged down. We have also been blessed by Viviana Velie and Editorial JUCUM, our Spanish-language publisher, whose belief in the importance of this book for the Spanish-speaking world helped us through a particularly difficult time.

I wish to thank Elizabeth and Jill, my co-authors. It has been a distinct honor and joy to work together on this project with such passionate, wise, and godly women. I also wish to thank my friends at the Disciple Nations Alliance, Bob Moffitt, Dwight Vogt, Stephen Langa, and Hein VanWyk, and particularly my long-time friend and mentor, Darrow Miller, all of whom believed in the project and encouraged me along the way. I am also deeply indebted to my wife, Kim, whom I love with all my heart. Her passion to pursue God in marriage and family has had a profound impact on my life. Her vision to home educate our five children, Kaila, Jenna, Luke, Isaac, and Annelise, has been a remarkable grace to me and the kids. God has used my family in more ways that I can express to teach me what biblical marriage and fatherhood are all about. I also wish to thank my parents, Dale and Margaret, whom I deeply love. You have provided me with the truly priceless gift of modeling a godly marriage.

Soli Deo Gloria

Scott D. Allen

About Chrysalis International

Chrysalis International (http://www.chrysalisinternational.org) is a nonprofit educational institute that disciples Christian leaders in the nations who are called to break the cycle of ignorance and the poverty of biblical ideas in the Church by: 1) teaching the knowledge and application of biblical principles for education and self-government to transform the culture for Christ; and 2) publishing resources, such as AMO®, our enriched, principle-based curriculum for children. Our resources and courses of study are based on a nation-building model that lays Christ and His Word as the foundation for renewing the mind, building a biblical, Christian worldview, and inspiring fresh vision for individual, family, and community transformation.

About the Disciple Nations Alliance

Disciple Nations Alliance (http://www.disciplenations.org/) is a movement comprised of individuals, churches, and organizations that are drawn together by a common vision: *To see the global Church rise to her full potential as God's instrument for the healing, blessing, and transformation of the nations.* DNA works to develop, promote, and distribute a "school of thought" and tools for application centered around three interrelated themes: (1) The central and strategic role of the Church in society, (2) the power of biblical truth for cultural and social transformation, and (3) the need for churches to practice a wholistic, incarnational ministry. DNA also works to envision, train, and connect emerging and established strategic leaders to develop grass-roots models and real-world application.

ENDNOTES

CHAPTER 1

1   Noah Webster, *American Dictionary of the English Language.* (1828 facsimile ed). (San Franciso, Calif: Foundation for American Christian Education, 1967).

2   Steven Davis, *God, Reason, and Theistic Proofs* (Grand Rapids, Mich.: Eerdmans Publishing Company, 1997), 8.

3   *Webster's Encyclopedic Unabridged Dictionary of the English Language*, based on the first edition of *The Random House Dictionary of the English Language, the Unabridged Edition*, copyright © 1983.

4   *Collins English Dictionary—Complete & Unabridged 10th Edition*, 2009 © William Collins Sons & Co. Ltd. 1979, 1986 © HarperCollins Publishers 1998, 2000, 2003, 2005, 2006, 2007, 2009.

5   Phillip E. Johnson, foreword to *Total Truth: Liberating Christianity from its Cultural Captivity* by Nancy Pearcey (Wheaton, Ill.: Crossway, 2004), 11.

6   Nancy Pearcey, *Saving Leonardo: A Call to Resist the Secular Assault on Mind, Morals and Meaning*, (Nashville, Tenn.: B&H Publishing Group, 2010), 14.

7   Ibid., 9.

8   Richard Fry and D'Vera Cohn, "Living Together: The Economics of Cohabitation," Pew Research Center Social and Demographic Trends, June 27, 2011, 1, http://www.pewsocialtrends.org/2011/06/27/living-together-the-economics-of-cohabitation/.

9   D'Vera Cohn, "Love and Marriage," Pew Research Center Social and Demographic Trends, February 13, 2013, http://www.pewsocialtrends.org/2013/02/13/love-and-marriage/.

10   "The Decline of Marriage and Rise of New Families," Pew Research Center Social and Demographic Trends, November 18, 2010, 1, http://www.pewsocialtrends.org/2010/11/18/the-decline-of-marriage-and-rise-of-new-families/.

CHAPTER 2

11   Microsoft Office Word 2007, © 2006 Microsoft Corporation.

12   Webster.

13   E. Stanley Jones, *Victorious Living* (Minneapolis, Minn.: Summerside Press, 1936), 20.

14   John Piper, *This Momentary Marriage: A Parable of Permanence* (Wheaton, Ill.: Crossway Books, 2009), 21.

15   Homosexuality in Scripture is consistently portrayed as an abomination—the result of human rebellion against God and His creation order (see Romans 1:18–27).

16   Douglas Wilson, *Reforming Marriage* (Moscow, Idaho: Canon Press, 2012), 16.

17   G. L. Archer Jr., "Covenant," *Evangelical Dictionary of Theology, Second Edition*, (Grand Rapids, Mich.: Baker Book House Company, 2001), 299.

18   Piper, 24–26.

19   Piper, 30.

20   1 Corinthians 7:39; 2 Corinthians 6:14.

21   Douglas Wilson, 44.

22   Piper, 25.

23   Piper, 24–26.

24   "Born Again Christians Just as Likely to Divorce as Are Non-Christians," The
       Barna Group, September 8, 2004, http://www.barna.org/barna-update/article/
       5-barna-update/194-born-again-christians-just-as-likely-to-divorce-as-are-non-
       christians?q = divorce.

25   http://www.marriagesavers.org.

26   http://www.2equal1.com.

27   Wayne Grudem, *Politics According to the Bible* (Grand Rapids, Mich.: Zondervan,
       2010), 221.

28   "Marriage Provides Better Health," National Marriage Week USA, http://www.
       nationalmarriageweekusa.org/research/articles/9-marriage-provides-
       better-health.

29   Piper, 17.

CHAPTER 3

30   J. I. Packer, *Concise Theology: A Guide to Historic Christian Beliefs* (Wheaton,
       Ill.: Tyndale, 2001), 232.

31   Philip Lancaster, *Family Man, Family Leader: Biblical Fatherhood as the Key to a
       Thriving Family* (San Antonio, Tex.: The Vision Forum, Inc., 2003), 127–128.

32   Piper, *This Momentary Marriage*, 80.

33   Lancaster, 65–67.

34   Simone Weil, *The Need for Roots: Prelude to a Declaration of Duties toward
       Mankind* (Boston, Mass.: Beacon Press, 1952), quoted in *The Roots of American
       Order* by Russell Kirk, (LaSalle, Ill.: Open Court, 1974), 3.

35   Piper, 78.

36   Lancaster, 127–128.

37   Nancy Wilson, *Praise Her in the Gates: The Calling of Christian Motherhood*
       (Moscow, Idaho: Canon Press, 2000), 44.

38   Lancaster, 135–136.

39   Ibid, 244.

40   Piper, 89.

41   Rosalie J. Slater, *Teaching and Learning America's Christian History: The
       Principle Approach* (San Francisco, Calif.: Foundation for American Christian
       Education, 1965), 69.

42   Ibid, 91.

43   Lancaster, 94.

44   Piper, 90.

45   Ibid, 89.

46 Darrow Miller, *Nurturing the Nations: Reclaiming the Dignity and Divine Calling of Women in Building Healthy Cultures* (Downers Grove, Ill.: InterVarsity Press, 2012), 142.

47 Packer, 230.

48 Piper, 101.

49 Nancy Wilson, *Praise Her in the Gates*, 48.

50 Miller, 146.

51 Packer, 232.

52 See Proverbs 5:23; 13:24; 22:15; 23:13, 14; 29:15; Hebrews 12:6; 9–11; and Revelation 3:19.

CHAPTER 4

53 Lancaster, *Family Man, Family Leader*, 6.

54 Ibid, 15–16.

55 *Webster's Encyclopedic Unabridged Dictionary*, 1983.

56 Grudem, *Politics According to the Bible*, 40–41.

57 Nancy Wilson, *Praise Her in the Gates*, 19–20.

58 A helpful resource on this subject is John Piper, *What's the Difference: Manhood and Womanhood Defined According to the Bible* (Wheaton:Ill.: Crossway, 2009).

59 Psalm 127:3–5; Matthew 19:13–14.

60 See http://www.deomgraphicwinter.com for a sobering overview of recent demographic trends.

61 See the World Factbook published by the U.S. Central Intelligence Agency at https://www.cia.gov/library/publications/the-world-factbook/rankorder/2127rank.html.

Anguilla	1.75
Aruba	1.84
Barbados	1.68
Bermuda	1.97
Brazil	1.82
Cayman Islands	1.87
Chile	1.87
Costa Rica	1.92
Cuba	1.45
Nicaragua	2.08
Paraguay	2.06
Puerto Rico	1.64
Saint Kitts and Nevis	1.79
Saint Lucia	1.8
Trinidad and Tobago	1.72
Turks and Caicos Islands	1.7
United States	2.06
Virgin Islands	1.78
Anguilla	1.75

62   Lancaster, 130–131.

63   Ibid., 147.

64   Packer, *Concise Theology,* 233

65   Lancaster, 140–141.

66   Albert Mohler, "America's Educational Crisis–A Christian Response," August 17, 2004, http://www.albertmohler.com/2004/08/17/americas-educational-crisis-a-christian-response/.

67   Lancaster, 142.

68   Packer, 233.

69   Lancaster, 148.

CHAPTER 5

70   Webster.

71   Vocabulary and language usage change over time, but the Bible does not present human language as having developed from animal sounds. God spoke to Adam after He created him, and Adam understood and named all creatures!

72   James 3:5, 6; 4:4.

73   John Piper and Justin Taylor, eds., *The Power of Words and the Wonder of God* (Wheaton, Ill.: Crossway Books, 2009), 19.

74   Matthew 5:3–11.

75   James Strong, *Strong's Exhaustive Concordance* (Nashville, Tenn.: Crusade Bible Publishers, 1974).

CHAPTER 6

76   Matthew 18:1–5.

77   *The World Factbook,* Central Intelligence Agency, https://www.cia.gov/library/publications/the-world-factbook/rankorder/2127rank.html.

78   Genesis 1:27.

79   Genesis 11:30.

80   Genesis 15:4–5.

81   Genesis 1:26.

82   1 John 2:12.

83   Galatians 4:3; Ephesians 4:14; Proverbs 1:4.

84   Jeremiah 1:6.

85   Psalm 139:14–15.

86   Jeremiah 4:31; Isaiah 11:8; Isaiah 28:9; Esther 3:13; Psalm 8:2; 1 Samuel 17:56; Proverbs 1:4; Psalm 10:14; Isaiah 9:6; Isaiah 31:8.

87   1 Kings 13:1–3.

88   Jeremiah 1:4.

89   2 Kings 22:1.

90   Romans 5:12.

91   John 3:16.

92   Ephesians 1:17–18.

CHAPTER 7

93   In the United States, over 85 percent of Christian parents enroll their children in public/state schools.

94   Proverbs 1:7; Ecclesiastes 12:13.

95   Marvin Wilson, *Our Father Abraham*, (Grand Rapids, Mich.: Eerdmans, 1989).

96   "What Is the Torah?" About.com, http://judaism.about.com/od/judaismbasics/a/What-Is-The-Torah-Chumash.htm.

97   Deuteronomy 11:18.

98   Bob Moffitt, "Luke 2:52 and Human Development," sermon guide available at http://harvestfoundation.org.

99   Mark 6:3.

100 Luke 2:51.

101 Luke 2:49.

102 Arthur Dicken Thomas, Jr., "Profiles in Faith: Susanna Wesley," Knowing and Doing, Winter 2003, 1, http:// http://www.cslewisinstitute.org/webfm_send/499.

103 Hugh Price Hughes, *The Journal of John Wesley* (Chicago: Moody Press, 1951).

104 Ibid.

105 James Rose, *A Guide to American Christian Education* (Camarillo, Calif.: American Christian History Institute, 1987), 92.

CHAPTER 8

106 Webster.

107 Tedd Tripp, *Shepherding a Child's Heart*, (Wapwallopen, Pa: Shepherd Press, 1995) 22, 125.

108 Nehemiah 7:3.

109 John 10:10.

110 Genesis 2:7.

111 Romans 8:15–16.

112 Andrew Murray, *How to Bring Your Children to Christ* (Springdale, Ark.: Whitaker House, 1984).

113 Luke 6:27–28.

114 Proverbs 9:10.

115 John 5:39-40.

116 Isaiah 11:2.

117 Daniel 1:4.

118 Daniel 1:17.

119 Hebrews 12:9; Ephesians 6:4; Colossians 3:21.

120 Hebrews 12:10.

121 Webster.

122 Hannah More, *Hints Towards Forming the Character of the Young Princess* (India: Mallock Press, 1805, reprint 2010), 41.

123 Hebrews 13:5–6.

124 Hebrews 13:7.

125   Matthew 20:25–28.

126   *Character Sketches* (Oakbrook, Ill.: Institute in Basic Life Principles, 1978).

127   Elizabeth L. Youmans, Evie Tindall, and Helen E. Wood, "Fantasy and the Imagination," *AMO® Apprenticeship Manual* (Orlando, Fla.: Chrysalis International, 2011), 214.

128   2 Corinthians 3:18.

129   Alexander Thomas and Stella Chess, *Temperament and Development* (Oxford: Brunner/Mazel, 1977), 21–22.

130   Ephesians 2:10.

131   1 Timothy 3:2; 1 Timothy 3:11; Titus 2:2.

132   Daniel 1:4.

133   Psalm 136:5.

134   *Mishnah*, Kiddushin 4:14; Matthew 13:55; Mark 6:3.

135   Proverbs 31:13–24.

136   1 Samuel 18:6; Luke 15:25.

137   1 Corinthians 12:7.

138   1 Corinthians 13:1–2.

139   1 Corinthians 14:12.

140   Chuck Colson, "Any Ol' World View Won't Do," Jubilee Newsletter Vol. IX, No. 8, September 1996, http://www.baptistbanner.org/Subarchive_8/896%20Any%20Ol'%20World%20View.htm.

141   Dan Smithwick, "Where Are We Going," Nehemiah Institute, August 1, 2008, http://www.nehemiahinstitute.com/articles/index.php?action=show&id=35.

142   Romans 12:2.

143   Voddie Baucham, *Family Driven Faith* (Wheaton, Ill.: Crossway, 2007), 74.

144   Philip Carrington, *The Primitive Christian Catechism* (Cambridge: University Press, 1940), 13.

145   Charles Colson and Nancy Pearcey, *How Now Shall We Live?* (Wheaton, Ill.: Tyndale, 2004).

146   http://www.thetruthproject.org/.

147   See chapter two for a more thorough discussion of male and female characteristics, roles, and functions.

148   Matthew 19:5–6; Mark 10:6–8.

149   Ephesians 5:31; 1 Corinthians 6:16.

150   Psalm 139:13.

151   Galatians 3:28.

152   1 Corinthians 6:9–11; Isaiah 53:4–5; Matthew 8:16–17; 1 Peter 2:24.

153   Nehemiah 9:38.

CHAPTER 9

154   Genesis 1:27.

155   Genesis 5:3.

156   Genesis 15–17.

157   Acts 3:25.

158   Exodus 12:1–12.

159   1 Corinthians 5:7.

160   Genesis 22:1–13.

161   Genesis 26:25; 35:1–7.

162   Webster.

163   John 14:15.

164   ¹¹ Timothy Keller, *Counterfeit Gods: The Empty Promises of Money, Sex, and Power, and the Only Hope That Matters* (New York: Dutton, 2009), xviii.

165   Psalm 97:7.

166   1 Timothy 6:10.

167   Daniel 3:5; 2 Kings 10:19; Isaiah 44:15.

168   Habakkuk 2:19.

169   In some cultures, these may include actual physical altars or idols (images, symbols, art) which much be destroyed. See Deuteronomy 12:3; 2 Kings 23:13; Psalm 101:3; Jeremiah 16:18.

170   Psalm 50:23a.

171   Colossians 3:16.

172   Psalm 22:3.

173   James 4:8.

174   1 Corinthians 14:26.

175   1 Corinthians 15:3–4.

176   Isaiah 55:9.

177   Romans 12:2.

178   John 11:42.

179   James 4:2b, 26; James 5:16; 1 John 1:9; 1 John 5:14–15; Psalm 66:18; Matthew 7:7–8; Luke11:13, John 14:13–14; Philippians 4:6–7; Hebrews 4:15, 16; Hebrews 10:19–22.

CHAPTER 11

180   Bob Moffitt, *The Discipline of Love* lesson overview, http://harvestfoundation. org/503746.ihtml

APPENDIX III

181   The list was identified as "God's One Anothers" by the Linwood Methodist Church of Kansas City, Missouri. *AMO® Apprenticeship Manual* (Orlando: Chrysalis International, 2011), 171–2.